Uncover 4

Workbook with Digital Pack

Lynne Robertson

CAMBRIDGE
UNIVERSITY PRESS

University Printing House, Cambridge CB2 8BS, United Kingdom

One Liberty Plaza, 20th Floor, New York, NY 10006, USA

477 Williamstown Road, Port Melbourne, VIC 3207, Australia

314–321, 3rd Floor, Plot 3, Splendor Forum, Jasola District Centre, New Delhi – 110025, India

103 Penang Road, #05–06/07, Visioncrest Commercial, Singapore 238467

Cambridge University Press is part of the University of Cambridge.

It furthers the University's mission by disseminating knowledge in the pursuit of education, learning and research at the highest international levels of excellence.

www.cambridge.org
Information on this title: www.cambridge.org/9781107493643

First published 2015

20 19 18 17

Printed in Great Britain by CPI Group (UK) Ltd, Croydon CRO 4YY

A catalog record for this publication is available from the British Library.

ISBN 978-1-107-49364-3 Workbook with Digital Pack 4

Additional resources for this publication at www.cambridge.org/uncover

Cambridge University Press has no responsibility for the persistence or accuracy of URLs for external or third-party Internet Web sites referred to in this publication and does not guarantee that any content on such Web sites is, or will remain, accurate or appropriate. Information regarding prices, travel timetables, and other factual information given in this work is correct at the time of first printing but Cambridge University Press does not guarantee the accuracy of such information thereafter.

Art direction, book design, layout services, and photo research: QBS Learning

Table of Contents

1 *Tell Me About It!*

1 Label the pictures with the correct words. One word is used more than once.

article	interview	the news	reporter
blogger	headline	paper	review

1. _____

2. _____

3. _____

4. _____

5. _____

6. _____

7. _____

8. _____

9. _____

2 Circle the correct answers.

Gina: Have you seen the ¹**article** / **news** yet?

Felix: No, what happened?

Gina: That ²**interview** / **reporter** you like quit. There's a new person reporting the news now.

Felix: Oh, well. I have to watch a ³**paper** / **report** every night because we talk about current events in my civics class.

Gina: Do you have to watch TV news? There's a ⁴**blogger** / **paper** I really like. He writes about interesting issues on his website.

Felix: Well, we're supposed to discuss local news in class. I can just read the local ⁵**paper** / **review**.

Gina: It's online, too, you know. Here, look. The ⁶**interview** / **headline** says that some roads will be closed this weekend. And there's an ⁷**interview** / **review** with the local police explaining what alternate routes to take.

Felix: That's kind of dull. The paper has this ⁸**blogger** / **article** about an old building the city wants to tear down, but some people want to preserve it. The mayor is holding a town hall meeting to discuss the issue on Friday.

Gina: That's a good issue to talk about in your class. Oh, look! There's a ⁹**review** / **headline** of the latest *Star Wars* movie. It opens this Friday. We should go!

Felix: Sure, we can go after the town hall meeting.

3 Answer the questions. Use your own information.

1. Where do you get the news?

   I get the news from the radio and online.

   _____

2. Where do your parents or grandparents get the news?

   _____

3. What kind of news articles do you like to read?

   _____

4. What kind of reviews interest you?

   _____

5. What is an interesting interview you have seen or heard?

   _____

Simple past, past continuous, and present perfect

1 Complete the chart.

Simple past

What _did_ you _watch_?

I _____ (watch) a news report online.

I _____ (not watch) it on television.

What _____ the reporter _____ (say)?

He _____ (say) the storm caused the power to go out.

But he _____ (not say) how long it would be out.

Past continuous

What _____ you _____ (do) when the power went out?

I **was driving** my car. I _____ (not use) my cell phone. That's dangerous.

Present perfect

Who **has seen** that new reality series?

I _____ (not see) it yet. But Laura _____ (see) every episode. She loves it.

---

2 Write each sentence in the simple past and in the past continuous.

1. Juan works at the store on weekends.

   Juan worked at the store on weekends.

   Juan was working at the store on weekends.

2. Jenny rides a bike in the morning.

   Jenny _____.

   Jenny _____.

3. Tom and Gina study Chinese.

   _____

   _____

4. We don't play football in the park.

   _____

   _____

3 Look at Exercise 2. Complete the questions and answers with the present perfect forms of the verbs.

1. **A:** Who ___ _has learned_ ___ (learn) how to read Chinese?

   B: _Tom and Gina have learned how to read Chinese._

2. **A:** Who _____ (work) on weekends before?

   B: _____

3. **A:** Who _____ (ride) a bike in the morning?

   B: _____

4. **A:** Who _____ (not play) football in the park?

   B: _____

Past passive and present perfect passive

4 Complete the chart.

Past passive

The article ___ _was posted_ ___ (post) online.

The photographs _____ (post) last week. But they _____ (not post) by me.

Present perfect passive

The video _has been watched_ (watch) by over 3 million people!

It _____ (see) in over 30 countries. But it _____ (not see) in the artist's own country.

---

5 Rewrite the sentences. Use the forms in parentheses.

1. Someone used a fact-checking site to prove that the legend was false. (past passive)

   A fact-checking site was used to prove that the

   legend was false.

2. No one posted the game scores to the school website. (present perfect passive)

   _____

3. Over 60,000 people attended the summer music festival. (past passive)

   _____

4. A cell phone didn't record the event. (present perfect passive)

   _____

VOCABULARY Time expressions

1 Read the sentences. Then circle the action that started or happened first.

1. My dad was living in a small town **before** he met my mother.

   a. (My dad lived in a small town)

   b. He met my mother.

2. **After** they got married, they moved to the city.

   a. They got married.

   b. They moved to the city.

3. My dad was working as a reporter **while** my mom was finishing college.

   a. He worked as a reporter.

   b. She finished college.

4. She got a job as a computer programmer **as soon as** she finished college.

   a. She got a job as a computer programmer.

   b. She finished college.

5. I was born **by the time** my mom was 30.

   a. I was born.

   b. My mom was 30.

6. She's been working part-time **since** I was born.

   a. She worked part-time.

   b. I was born.

7. **Whenever** I had a question about my computer homework, she helped me.

   a. I had a question about my computer homework.

   b. She helped me.

8. **Every time** there's been a new smartphone, she's been the first to try it.

   a. There's a new smartphone.

   b. She was the first to try it.

2 Complete the sentences with the correct words.

1. *As soon as* I wake up in the morning, I take a shower. (As soon as / By the time)

2. _____ he eats breakfast, my dad checks his email. (Until / While)

3. He rode his bike to school _____ he learned to drive. (every time / until)

4. She's been playing video games _____ she was six. (since / whenever)

5. _____ I go to school in the morning, I charge my phone battery. (Before / Since)

6. _____ I got the text, I had already left. (By the time / Every time)

7. _____ I use the school computer, I forget to sign out. (As / Every time)

8. Hannah texted me _____ the game had finished. (after / whenever)

9. _____ I was researching my paper online, I saw the headlines on a news website. (As / Until)

10. _____ my smartphone rings in class, my teacher gets angry. (Before / Whenever)

11. There was nobody in the library _____ I left last night. (when / as soon as)

3 Use the time expressions from Exercise 1 to combine sentences. More than one answer may be possible.

1. My laptop broke. I was watching my friend's video clips.

   My laptop broke while I was

   watching my friend's video clips.

2. The game had ended. I texted my dad.

   _____

3. I bought tickets for the concert. They went on sale at noon.

   _____

4. The band was playing their last song. I recorded it with my smartphone.

   _____

5. I studied for the test. I was taking the bus to school.

   _____

GRAMMAR Review of *used to* + infinitive and *would*

1 Read the sentences and check (✓) the correct columns.

	Thing that happened repeatedly in the past but doesn't happen now	Situation that happened in the past
1. I used to live on a houseboat when I was a baby.		✓
2. My brother used to study German.		
3. Jack would always win when we played tennis.		
4. I would watch the news at night.		
5. My family didn't use to own a television.		
6. I didn't use to like to eat vegetables.		

2 Complete the conversation. Use *used to*, *would*, or the simple past. More than one answer may be possible.

Marissa: Hey, Gan. Where in Thailand ¹ *did you use to* live when you were young?

Gan: Well, when I was very young, I ² _____ in Bangkok. We lived on a *khlong*, or canal.

Marissa: Interesting. Did you ³ _____ swimming a lot?

Gan: No! We never ⁴ _____ go in the water.

Marissa: ⁵ _____ you go fishing?

Gan: No, we ⁶ _____. But my family ⁷ _____ go to the floating market.

Marissa: What ⁸ _____ you buy at the market?

Gan: We ⁹ _____ buy fruit and vegetables. And we ¹⁰ _____ eat dinner from kitchens on the boats and drink coconut drinks.

Marissa: How often ¹¹ _____ eat at the market?

Gan: We ¹² _____ eat there a couple times a week. It was fun.

3 Correct the sentences. Use *used to*, *would*, or the simple past. More than one answer may be possible.

played
1. Kevin ~~would play~~ in the snow last vacation.
2. We would live in Hawaii when I was younger.
3. My grandparents didn't used to use their new computer until I showed them how.
4. I used to play my video game at 8:00 last night.
5. My family was buying vegetables at the store until we started our garden.

4 Answer the questions using *used to* or *would*. Use your own information.

1. Where did you live when you were young?

   _____

   _____

2. What music did you listen to when you were young?

   _____

   _____

3. What games did you play with your friends?

   _____

   _____

4. What movies or TV shows did you watch?

   _____

   _____

1 Put the words in the correct order to make sentences.

1. right / really / the / I'm / playing / into / guitar / now / .

   I'm really into playing the guitar right now.

2. crazy / live / I'm / not / about / music / .

   _____

3. I'm / that / into / not / music videos / watching / .

   _____

4. all / bands / I'm / about / punk / .

   _____

5. stand / music / I / can't / pop / .

   _____

6. about / I'm / new / this / video / crazy / .

   _____

2 Complete the conversation with the correct phrases. More than one answer may be possible.

✓all about	crazy about	not that into
can't stand	not crazy about	really into

Paul: Have you watched my new music video yet?

Ellie: No, I haven't. Sorry. I'm [1] *all about* this new John Mayer video right now.

Paul: Ugh! I [2] _____ him!

Ellie: Really? But he plays guitar, like you.

Paul: Yeah, but we play different kinds of music. I like alternative and punk. I'm [3] _____ his singer-songwriter sound.

Ellie: Oh, well. How about Ellie Goulding? I'm [4] _____ her this year. She's amazing!

Paul: Her music and voice are OK, but I'm [5] _____ her like you are. She's still too pop for me.

Ellie: Oh, are you still [6] _____ Green Day?

Paul: Of course! They're my favorite!

1 Number the parts of an informational blog post in order from 1–4.

_____ Give details about what you did or saw.   _____ Give general information about the event.

_____ Give information about the event in the future   _____ Give your opinion about the event.
or similar events.

2 Use Exercise 1 to number the parts of this informational blog post in order from 1–4.

BATTLE OF THE BANDS | Lake High School

by Hailey Morgan

_____ Battle of the Bands takes place twice during the school year. The next one takes place in early January. Finalists go to the state finals in April.

_____ I went to Battle of the Bands at our high school last Saturday. It's an event for local high school bands to compete to win. The audience votes by cheering loudly for their favorite band. So it's up to the audience themselves to make some noise for the winner.

_____ I thought the band that won, The Closers, was really good. But I'm not that into rock and roll. I was crazy about the all-girl rap band, Tiger Lily. They were awesome. I myself would like to try rapping!

_____ Before the bands played, the school band played a song. Then the bands came out. Each band got to play three songs. After a band was done, the drama club performed a dance or comedy act while the next band set up. They really challenged themselves with some crazy dancing this year! The whole event took about three hours.

3 Find the examples of reflexive and emphatic pronouns in Hailey's blog. Underline the reflexive pronouns. Circle the emphatic ones.

4 Read the blog post in Exercise 2 again. Answer the questions.

1. What was the event?

   The event was Battle of the Bands.

2. When was it?

   _____

3. Where was it?

   _____

4. Who competes?

   _____

5. How do they win?

   _____

6. Who won the contest?

   _____

7. Which band did Hailey like?

   _____

Best Foot Forward

2

VOCABULARY Personal qualities

1 Find nine more words for personal qualities.

B	L	H	Q	S	T	R	I	C	T	T	J
I	E	A	S	Y	G	O	I	N	G	R	W
P	X	R	L	F	S	F	T	I	D	C	A
A	R	D	O	G	C	V	Z	S	E	Q	B
S	J	W	M	O	T	I	V	A	T	E	D
S	S	O	I	M	P	A	T	I	E	N	T
I	H	R	U	G	F	H	F	N	R	J	V
O	Y	K	O	O	Z	C	S	H	M	U	C
N	V	I	D	R	R	L	T	C	I	N	A
A	J	N	B	P	Z	A	G	S	N	G	R
T	S	G	T	A	L	E	N	T	E	D	B
E	S	O	C	I	A	B	L	E	D	I	D

2 Complete the conversation with the correct words from Activity 1. More than one answer may be possible.

Tim: I think Kyla can win the singing competition. She's very ¹___*passionate*___ and you can hear it in her voice. And she's
²_____, too. It just seems easy for her to sing beautifully. She doesn't have to try as hard as everyone else.

Amy: Yes, but John has a chance to win the competition, too. It's not as easy for him, but he is very ³_____ to improve. And he spends all of his time practicing the same song over and over. He is very
⁴_____.

Tim: Yeah, well, John can't make any mistakes because his coach is so ⁵_____. On top of that, the coach is ⁶_____, so John has to learn quickly.

Amy: Well, you know who needs a tougher coach? Noah! He doesn't try hard enough. He is too ⁷_____. It's lucky he's ⁸_____ and chats with the judges. They like him for that.

Tim: What about Callie? She's the opposite of Noah. She's so ⁹_____ that she never chats with the judges.

Amy: You're right. And she's so afraid of making mistakes, it seems like she almost doesn't care about winning. The judges don't like it when you don't show that you're ¹⁰_____. I think she'll go home next.

3 Answer the questions with the words from Exercise 1 and your own information.

1. Describe someone you know who is easy-going.

   My friend Alicia is easy-going. She doesn't
   get upset about anything. She acts the same
   if she gets a good or bad grade on a test.

2. Do you know someone who is talented? What is he or she good at?

   _____

3. Do you know someone who is hard-working? What makes him or her hard-working?

   _____

4. Name two personal qualities that you have. Describe them.

   _____

   _____

5. Describe two personal qualities you wish you had. How would these qualities help you?

   _____

   _____

GRAMMAR Present perfect with present perfect continuous

1 Put the words in the correct order to make sentences.

1. surfing / He / time / been / long / for / hasn't / a / .

   He hasn't been surfing for a long time.

2. hours / been / three / for / chatting / online / We've / !

   _____

3. been / since / Ella's / making / 2011 / films / .

   _____

4. watching / I / been / lately / haven't / movies / any / .

   _____

5. to / running, / but / I / now / love / stopped / I've / running / used / .

   _____

6. haven't / since / rock climbing / 2013 / They / been / .

   _____

2 Look at Helen's timeline. Complete the questions and answers using the present perfect or the present perfect continuous form of the verbs.

live in England   work as a journalist

2010 2011 2012 2013 2014 2015 NOW

study Portuguese   move to Brazil

learn to sail

1. **Kay:** Helen, ___*have*___ you *been living* (live) in England?

   Helen: No, I _____ . I _____ in Brazil.

2. **Kay:** _____ you _____ (sail) for a long time?

   Helen: No, I _____ . I _____ since 2014.

3. **Kay:** _____ you _____ (work) as a journalist for a long time?

   Helen: Not really. I _____ as a journalist since 2013.

4. **Mike:** What _____ Helen _____ doing lately?

   Kay: She _____ (work) as a journalist.

5. **Mike:** _____ Helen _____ (study) Spanish?

   Kay: No, she _____ . She _____ Portuguese.

3 Rewrite the sentences. Change the present perfect to the present continuous or the present continuous to the present perfect, when possible. Write X if the sentence can't be rewritten.

1. She has never ~~been seeing~~ a Broadway show.

   She has never seen a Broadway show.

2. I've played football for a long time.

   _____

3. Stacy has wanted to buy a car for a long time.

   _____

4. Gavin has been working at the law firm for 10 years.

   _____

5. Ellen has been in Paris since Tuesday.

   _____

4 Answer the questions. Use your own information.

1. Have you ever studied Russian?

   _____

2. Where have you been studying English?

   _____

3. What have you been doing lately?

   _____

4. What is something you've never done?

   _____

5. How long have you known your best friend?

   _____

VOCABULARY Phrasal verbs about making progress

1 Complete the sentences with a word from each box. Use the correct verb forms.

bring	pass	along	up
count	set	into	up
get	sign	on	up
~~give~~	turn	on	together
keep		~~up~~	

1. Our team is losing, but they're determined. They won't ___*give up*___ .

2. The new website has _____ different music fans from all over the world.

3. Marla is so nice that she can _____ with anyone.

4. I helped my grandparents _____ their social networking page.

5. They find it difficult to _____ with all of the latest technology.

6. The organization started small, but it's _____ a global success.

7. Some people worry that they won't be able to _____ their traditions to their grandchildren.

8. Let's _____ to help at the beach clean up.

9. John is always there for you. You can _____ him to help you.

2 Correct the sentences if needed. Write ✓ if they are already correct.

1. It took 10 minutes to set her new smartphone up. __✓__

2. Millie's so motivated! She's already signed for dance lessons up. _____

3. We've been trying to get with the other team along. _____

4. My dream is to be a writer, and I don't want to give it up. _____

5. That new app has brought some very different people together. _____

6. The organization has a great program to pass used clothing along to people who need it. _____

7. His hobby has turned his career into. _____

8. I don't have time to keep with my social networking up. _____

9. Who can you count for a ride tonight on? _____

3 Complete the conversation with some of the phrasal verbs from Exercise 1. Use the correct verb forms.

Andrea: Have you [1] _____ for the race yet?

Bill: No, I haven't. I know it's a great event that [2] _____ a lot of people _____, but I don't think I can run that far. I'll [3] _____ before I get to the end.

Andrea: Bill! Don't [4] _____ this _____ a big drama! It's just a fun run. I don't run that fast, and I'm doing it. You can [5] _____ with me, can't you?

Bill: I don't know . . .

Andrea: Look, you can run with our running group twice a week. We'll [6] _____ a training program for you. And Ken is training with us, too, you know. I know you [7] _____ well with him.

Bill: Ken's doing the run? Oh, OK. I'll do it.

Andrea: Thanks, Bill! I knew I could [8] _____ you!

GRAMMAR Past perfect and past perfect continuous

1 Read the sentences. Circle the answer that correctly explains each situation.

1. Tina and Mel had been in Africa when the program started.

   a. The program started during their time in Africa

   b. The program started before they went to Africa.

2. They hadn't been checking their email as often during the program.

   a. They used to check their email regularly before the program.

   b. They didn't use to check their email regularly before the program.

3. The band had been touring since 2010.

   a. They probably toured for a few years and stopped.

   b. They toured and are probably still touring.

4. Sophia had been volunteering at the center for six months.

   a. Sophia is probably still volunteering at the center.

   b. Sophia is probably doing something else now.

5. People had been signing up for the service over the weekend.

   a. It is still the weekend now.

   b. It is some time after the weekend now.

2 Complete the sentences and questions with the words in parentheses. Use the past perfect continuous.

1. They _had been practicing_ (practice) their new song when the power went out.

2. Tara and Milo _____ (exchange) emails.

3. Their concerts _____ (sell out) quickly.

4. My sister _____ (not study) the piano.

5. We _____ (talk) for hours and hadn't realized the time.

3 Look at Mai's activities. Complete the sentences with the past perfect and past perfect continuous.

study dance in Chicago	six years
live in Los Angeles	2011–2013
compete in a television dance show	June 2012
sing and dance in a movie	Summer 2013
move to New York City	October 2013
record an album	2014

1. Mai _____had studied_____ dance in Chicago for six years.

2. Mai _____ in a dance show before she moved to New York City.

3. She _____ in Los Angeles when she went on TV.

4. Mai _____ in a movie before she moved to New York City.

5. Mai _____ an album in 2014.

4 Put the words in the correct order to make questions. Answer the questions.

1. in / Mai been / Chicago / studying / dance / Had / ?

   Had Mai been studying dance in Chicago?

   Yes, she had.

2. when / recording / Mai been / she / in / Had / Los Angeles / an album / lived / ?

   _____

   _____

3. to / had / she / moved / Mai been / What / doing / before / New York City / ?

   _____

   _____

4. living / been / Where / 2012 / Mai / in / had / ?

   _____

   _____

CONVERSATION Showing concern

1 Match the phrases to make expressions to show concern.

1. I'm sorry   a. all right?

2. What's the   b. anything I can do?

3. I hope   c. matter?

4. What's   d. to hear that.

5. Are you   e. things get better.

6. Is there   f. wrong with her?

2 Use the phrases from Exercise 1 to complete the conversation.

Ilona: Hey, Julio. ¹ *Are you all right?*

Julio: I'm OK, I guess.

Ilona: No, you're not. You look tired.
² _____

Julio: Well, I'm worried about my mother.

Ilona: ³ _____

Julio: Oh, nothing's wrong with her. In fact, just the opposite. Ever since we got a new puppy, she's been so energetic.

Ilona: Who's been energetic? Your mom or the puppy?

Julio: Actually, both of them! My mom gets up really early to take the puppy out in the morning. Then, after school, she takes it jogging. And she makes me come with her! That's why I look tired.

Ilona: Julio! That's not really a problem, is it?

Julio: No, but now she's talking about getting a second dog! I'm going to have to join the track team to keep up.

Ilona: That's funny. Well, at least your dog can run. My cat is really overweight. I'm worried about him.

Julio: ⁴ _____ . ⁵ _____ ?

Ilona: Thanks, but no. We're already doing everything we can to help him eat less and exercise more.

Julio: Well, ⁶ _____ . And if you ever want to come on a run with us, let me know!

Ilona: Thanks!

12 | Unit 2

READING TO WRITE

1 Complete Jenny's thank-you email with the correct words.

Bye for now	I've attached
~~Hi,~~	Thanks
I'm writing to thank you for	Thank you for

000

To: MToth@cup.net
From: JennyPalooza@cup.net
Subject: Thank you!

¹_____ *Hi* _____, Ms. Toth,

²_____ being a great art teacher. Since graduating from high school, I've gone to college and I've been studying art. You really motivated me to work harder. Sometimes in class, I look at the other students' work and think they are more talented than me. But then I immediately remember you used to tell me to just be myself and do the work. Gradually, I've been feeling better about my work. ³_____ that.

I also want to let you know that the oil paints you gave me as a gift have been wonderful! Since I got them, I've been painting much better. I like them more than the watercolors I'd been using. ⁴_____ so much for them! ⁵_____ a photo of my latest painting. I hope you like it!

⁶_____ , Jenny

2 Read the letter in Exercise 1 again. Write the phrases next to each section below.

A greeting: _____ *Hi, Ms. Toth* _____

A reason for writing: _____

Details: _____

_____

A closing: _____

Sending a photo: _____

3 Read the letter in Exercise 1 again. Answer the questions.

1. What was Jenny doing before college?

_____

2. What phrase in Jenny's email helped you to answer question 1?

_____

3. How do Jenny's thoughts change during class?

_____

4. What phrase helped you to answer question 3?

_____

5. What change has happened for Jenny?

_____

6. What word explains that this change has happened to Jenny slowly, over time?

_____

7. Which word explains something that happened after Jenny was given a gift?

_____

8. What has changed for Jenny since she received the gift?

_____

REVIEW UNITS 1–2

1 Complete the chart.

article.   interview   review
blogger   motivated   sociable
impatient   reporter

Media	People	Personal qualities
article		

2 Complete each sentence with a word from each box. Use the correct verb forms.

count.	along
get	into
give	on.
keep	up
set	up
turn	up

1. I used to _count on_ Ella to help me with my homework.

2. I was having trouble _____ with my teammates during the race.

3. His experience writing blog posts _____ a job as a journalist.

4. They got a new laptop, and now they're _____ a new social networking page.

5. Last year, I _____ well with all my classmates.

6. I didn't have enough time to study until I _____ watching television.

3 Complete the sentences with *would* when possible. If not possible, use *used to*.

1. I _used to_ listen to hip hop, but now I listen to rock.

2. We _____ watch movies every night, but now we only watch them on weekends.

3. He was so shy, he _____ stay at home every night until he joined our club.

4. Jill _____ ride her bike to school, and now she rides it to work.

5. The organization _____ have a big party every year to thank the volunteers.

6. _____ you listen to the radio every night?

4 Circle the correct answers.

1. **Ben:** Who (did) / was you (interview) / interviewed for the school blog?

   Max: I **was interviewing / interviewed** Coldplay!

2. The album **was recording / was recorded** in the studio. It **wasn't recorded / wasn't recording** while the band was on tour.

3. **Mia:** Where **was / were** you **watched / watching** the news report?

   Sara: I **was watching / have watched** it online. I **wasn't watching / haven't watched** it on television.

4. **Jen:** Who **has been / was going** to Rome before?

   Chris: Danielle **has been / was going** to Rome. I think she **has been / went** last May.

5. The interview **was playing / has been played** on the radio twice today. But it **didn't post / hasn't been posted** on the web page yet.

5 Correct the sentences.

doing
1. What have you been ~~do~~ at the volunteer center?

2. Mara been knowing Lauren since she was five.

3. I have spending three months in Chile this past year.

4. You haven't been post on your web page lately.

5. Elliot was working as a volunteer for two years, but he's running the organization now.

6. They're not having worked late for a long time.

6 Complete the blog post with the words in parentheses. Use the correct verb forms.

GETTING READY FOR MY TRIP!

by Emily

I'm really into Mongolian throat singing lately.
I [1] *had been taking* (take) singing lessons for about fives years before I learned about Mongolian throat singing.
I [2]_____ (not hear) of that kind of singing before. It's an amazing sound because the singer sings two or more sounds at the same time.

Mongolian throat singing [3] _____ (be) around for a long time. Historically, men
[4]_____ (be) the majority of throat singers, but more women
[5]_____ (learn) to do it lately.
I [6]_____ (work) with a singing coach to practice Mongolian singing, when she told me about a singing camp in Mongolia.
I [7]_____ (sign up) right away. It's in Siberia, and most people speak Russian. So, after I
[8]_____ (sign up) to go, I started taking Russian lessons, too.
I [9]_____ (use) my voice a lot lately! I'm so excited for my trip! I leave next month!

7 Complete the conversation. More than one answer may be possible.

can't stand	not crazy about
crazy about	not that into
Is there anything I can do?	~~What's the matter?~~

Lukas: Hey, Tatiana. You look upset.
[1] *What's the matter?*

Tatiana: Oh, it's nothing important. It's just that Tim got us tickets to go to a car race this weekend.

Lukas: Well, that sounds fun!

Tatiana: Not for me! I [2]_____ car racing! It's so noisy! I told him I wanted to go to the beach.

Lukas: Really? I'm [3]_____ car racing!

Tatiana: Ugh. I'm [4]_____ it. And I'm [5]_____ spending my weekend at the race.

Lukas: [6]_____

Tatiana: Yeah, actually there is. Maybe you can go with him to the race instead!

8 Put the words in the correct order to make sentences. Then use the sentences to complete the conversation.

her / with / wrong / What's / ?
~~you / Raul / all / right, / Are / ?~~
I / hear / hope / from / you / Well, / her / .
into / really / organic farming / She's / .
sorry / hear / I'm / that / to / Oh, / .

Liana: [1] *Are you all right, Raul?*

Raul: Not really. I'm worried about my sister.

Liana: [2]_____

Raul: She's in Peru. I haven't heard from her in a while.

Liana: What's she been doing there?

Raul: [3]_____ So she's been volunteering at a farm in the Amazon jungle. But the last I heard from her, she wasn't feeling well.

Liana: [4]_____ Well, maybe their power is out or something.

Raul: Yeah, maybe.

Liana: [5]_____

Raul: Thanks.

3 Planning for the Future

1 Unscramble the verbs used to talk about the future.

1. e o m v _____*move*_____

2. n a p l _____

3. w r g o p u _____

4. e p k e n o _____

5. d e g a t r u a _____

6. e c m b e o _____

7. d e n p u _____

8. t r i p e c d _____

2 Complete the sentences with the phrases from Exercise 1. Use the correct verb forms.

1. Jason is good at art. I _____*predict*_____ he'll study painting in college.

2. I really enjoy playing the guitar. I have to _____ practicing so I can play in a band.

3. After I _____ to London, I hope to get a job at a start-up company.

4. Ellen wants to take a year off and travel after she _____ from high school.

5. He's not _____ to work for a company after college. He wants to start his own business!

6. My nine-year-old sister loves animals. She can't wait to _____ and become a veterinarian.

7. If you don't work toward your goals, you'll _____ doing nothing.

8. He studied music for many years before he _____ a professional musician.

3 Complete Julian's email with some of the expressions from Exercise 1. Use the correct verb forms.

To Mariano_M@cambridge.edu
From JulianCompU@cambridge.edu
Subject Hello!

Dear Mr. Mariano,

How are you? I haven't talked to you since I ¹___*graduated*___ from high school! I wanted to update you on what I've been doing and what I'm ²_____ for the future.

As you know, I'm in college and I've been studying computers. It's difficult, but I will ³_____ studying until computer science ⁴_____ easier for me!

I ⁵_____ that I will graduate in four more years. After that, I think I will ⁶_____ to San Francisco and will probably ⁷_____ working for a computer game company.

You know, computer games have been a big part of my life. When I was little, I told myself, "When I ⁸_____, I will make games that kids love to play." And now, I'm working on that goal! Anyway, I wanted you to know that I really appreciated your computer class in high school!

Sincerely,

Julian

4 Write statements about your future. Use the words in parentheses and your own information.

1. (plan)

   I plan on visiting a new country every year.

   _____

2. (become)

   _____

3. (keep on)

   _____

4. (end up)

   _____

GRAMMAR Future review

1 Complete the chart.

will for predictions	be going to for planned actions and events
1. What flight _____ Charlotte take? She'**ll** take the flight from London. She ____ _won't_ ____ take the one from Glasgow.	2. Who _____ she _____ visit? She _____ visit her cousins. She **isn't going to** visit her college friends.

Present continuous for planned actions and events	Simple present for scheduled future events
3. Which suitcase _____ she **taking** with her? She _____ the green suitcase. She **isn't taking** the brown one.	4. What **does** she _plan_ to see? She _____ to see the Met and a show on Broadway. She **doesn't** _____ to see Ellis Island.

2 Complete the sentences about Jorge's future plans. Circle the correct forms of the verbs.

1. Next weekend, Jorge ⟨**is going to**⟩/ **going** graduate from college. He **isn't going to / isn't going** keep on taking classes.

2. After graduating, Jorge **is going to plan / plans** to have a party at his house.

3. Jorge **will have / is having** a fun graduation party next weekend.

4. Next month, Jorge **will go / is going** to Peru.

5. Jorge **will / plans** to work at a non-profit organization in Peru.

6. He thinks he **will go / is going** to law school when he returns from Peru.

3 Use the chart to complete the questions and answers with future tenses. More than one answer may be possible.

	Planned actions	Planned events	Predictions
James	spend a month (August) in Paris	study at a French language school	travel in Europe in the fall
Rita	live in New York July – August	intern at a magazine	get hired by magazine in September

1. **Q:** Where _is_ James _planning_ to go in August?
   A: He'_s planning_ to go to Paris.

2. **Q:** What _____ James _____ in Paris?
   A: He's _____ French at a language school.

3. **Q:** What _____ James _____ in the fall?
   A: He _____ in Europe.

4. **Q:** When _____ Rita _____ in New York?
   A: She _____ there from July to August.

5. **Q:** What _____ she _____ to do there?
   A: She _____ to intern at a magazine.

6. **Q:** What _____ she _____ after that?
   A: She _____ by the magazine.

4 Answer the questions about a friend.

1. **Q:** What is your friend planning to do tomorrow?
   A: _____
   _____

2. **Q:** What will your friend do next weekend?
   A: _____
   _____

3. **Q:** What will your friend do next year?
   A: _____
   _____

VOCABULARY Achievements

1 Complete the phrases. Then match the pictures with the phrases.

1.	win	*an award*	c
2.		a business	
3.	do		
4.		a record	
5.	support		
6.		a million dollars	
7.		a project	
8.		famous	

a.
b.  Project Management

c.
d.

e.
f.

g.
h.

2 Answer the questions with the phrases from Exercise 1.

1. Which three achievements can relate to sports?

_____, _____,

and _____

2. Which three achievements most likely relate to a business?

_____, _____,

and _____

3. Which two achievements most likely help people?

_____ and _____

3 Complete the sentences with the correct form of phrases from Exercise 1. Then check (✓) if the sentences are true for you.

	True
1. I think ___*winning an award*___ for something you've done well is the best feeling.	
2. I want to _____ so I can support my family. It would be nice not to worry about money.	
3. I think that when people _____, they don't have any privacy. But it is still great because everyone knows who you are!	
4. If I _____, I can make the company's rules.	
5. I think people should _____ more often. There are always places to clean up or community projects that need help.	
6. I think anyone can _____. These days, you can raise money online to fund anything, even a movie you'd like to make!	
7. I want to work for an organization that _____. I think it's important to work locally to improve things.	
8. I think that if you practice and work hard, it's possible to _____ in any sport. But you have to really want to do it.	

4 Complete the questions with some of the phrases from Exercise 1. Then write answers that are true for you.

1. **Q:** Who do you think deserves to win _*an award*_ ?
   A: *I think Leonardo DiCaprio deserves to win an*
   award for donating money to save the oceans.

   _____

   _____

2. **Q:** Which of your friends do you think will become _____? Why?
   A: _____

3. **Q:** What kind of business would you like to _____?
   A: _____

4. **Q:** What kind of _____ work would you like to do?
   A: _____

5. **Q:** What record would you like to _____?

    A: _____

6. **Q:** If you _____ a million dollars, how will you spend it?

    A: _____

GRAMMAR Future continuous and future perfect

1 Complete the chart.

Use future continuous to describe something in progress in the future.	
1. Who _will_ be _supporting_ the race on Saturday? Our club _____ _____ the race on Saturday.	2. _____ Donny _____ volunteering at the beach clean up? No, he _____. But I will.

Use future perfect to describe something that is going to be finished at a certain time in the future.	
3. What _will_ your team _have_ developed by next year? We _____ _____ a community garden.	4. _____ Everett _____ a business by next year? Yes, he _____.

2 Change the sentences. Change the present continuous to the future continuous or future perfect.

1. Alex is volunteering with Kim next week.

   Alex will be volunteering with Kim next week.

2. They're collecting a million dollars by this time next month.

   _____

   _____

3. They're using the money they collect to do a community project.

   _____

   _____

4. By 2020, the project is helping over 1,000 children.

   _____

   _____

5. Rachel thinks the organization is winning an award for community service by 2017.

   _____

   _____

6. They're supporting community projects in Haiti.

   _____

   _____

3 Answer the questions with your own ideas. Use the future continuous or future perfect.

1. Which of your friends will have made a million dollars in the next 10 years?

   I think my friend Zack will have made a

   million dollars in the next 10 years. He's very

   hard-working.

   _____

   _____

2. Which of your friends do you think will be helping his/her community in the next two years?

   _____

   _____

3. Which of your friends will have traveled the most by 2025?

   _____

   _____

4. Which of your friends do you think will have started a business?

   _____

   _____

5. What will you be doing in 10 years?

   _____

   _____

1. Circle the correct answers.

1. The neighborhood created the community garden **as a result / (so that)** people would have access to fresh fruit and vegetables.

2. The shoe company has been donating 10 percent of its profits to charity, and **because of / consequently** their sales have gone up.

3. Pollution from plastic bags in the ocean has decreased **so that / thanks to** the new law that bans them.

4. Terry was able to save money for a new guitar **because of / since** his part-time job.

5. **Since / Consequently**, the number of people donating to the charity has increased, more projects are getting funded.

6. The benefit concert was a huge success, and **so that / as a result**, the class has earned enough money for a graduation party.

2 Complete the conversation with the phrases from Exercise 1. More than one answer may be possible.

Luis: Hi, Kathryn. ¹_____*Thanks to*_____ you, our after-school club will be getting two new laptops!

Kathryn: Really? What did I do?

Luis: ²_____ your article in the paper, some local businesses started a donation program. ³_____, they donated enough money for us to buy two new computers. Even the Senior Center donated!

Kathryn: Wow! You know, ⁴_____ they donated to us, maybe we should help them. We could take the laptops to the Senior Center and help the seniors to send emails and talk to their families. You know, do something nice for them ⁵_____ they know we appreciate what they did for us.

Luis: That's a fantastic idea!

1 **Complete Michelle's opinion essay with the correct words.**

For paragraph B:

consequently	~~For one thing.~~
inevitably	what's more

For paragraph C:

in addition	obviously
surely	therefore

Should soft drinks be sold *at School?*

by Michelle Leto

A What do you drink at lunch? Many schools in the United States have food and drinks for sale at lunchtime. Many schools have vending machines that sell soda. Personally, I don't think sodas or soft drinks with sugar in them should be sold at schools. Everyone knows by now that too much sugar isn't healthy.

B Why is sugar bad? [1] _*For one thing*_ , sugar has a lot of calories, but it does not provide any nutrients — the good things the body needs to stay healthy. [2] _____, the empty calories in sugar make people gain weight. [3] _____, eating sugar gives people a burst of energy at first, but then it makes them feel tired. Almost [4] _____, people then want to eat even more sugar.

C Research shows that people weigh more today than they did 50 years ago. [5] _____ to eating too much sugar, this is because people are not exercising enough. This is [6] _____ not healthy. Everyone can see that! [7] _____ something could be done to help get people interested in exercising. [8] _____, I think schools should require an hour of exercise every morning to music that students get to choose.

D Some people think that students should be able to make their own choices. I agree with that for some things. For example, I think it's important for students to be able to choose classes that prepare them for their chosen careers.

E But schools are meant to educate. So I think it's important to teach students to make better choices about their health.

2 **Read the article in Exercise 1 again. Write the paragraph letters next to each section below.**

___ A paragraph with arguments in favor

___ A conclusion

___ An introduction

___, ___ Paragraphs with arguments against

3 **Read the article in Exercise 1 again. Answer the questions.**

1. What does Michelle use to get the reader's attention?

_____

_____

2. What reasons does Michelle give against sugar?

_____

_____

3. What does Michelle say that schools should do to help students get more exercise?

_____

_____

4. What does Michelle think students should be allowed to choose?

_____

_____

4 What's Cooking?

1 Find eight more cooking verbs. Then label the pictures.

I	L	E	J	L	P	Z	K	W	S
B	F	W	S	R	O	A	S	T	P
E	R	D	G	R	I	L	L	R	L
S	Y	B	O	I	L	Z	W	N	J
L	B	P	C	H	I	V	Z	N	M
I	A	F	H	I	O	X	G	M	I
C	K	U	O	V	K	X	R	Y	X
E	E	W	P	S	J	N	A	C	U
M	I	U	J	I	T	Z	T	B	I
V	Q	T	H	H	K	T	E	M	T

1. _____roast_____   2. _____

3. _____   4. _____

5. _____   6. _____

7. _____   8. _____

9. _____

2 Complete Justin's email with some of the words from Exercise 1. Use the simple past.

○○○

Hi Wanda,

I am having a great time at chef school! It's more difficult than I expected, but I'm learning a lot. Did you know that we had a whole lesson just learning how to ¹ **boil** water? And then we spent an entire week just learning knife skills, such as how to ² _____ meat and how to ³ _____ onions into little pieces. That lesson made me cry! Ha ha!

It's funny. I thought I knew the basics of how to cook, but since coming here, I've already learned so much! For instance, I now know why the skin turns brown on top when you ⁴ _____ a chicken, and why the dough rises when you ⁵ _____ bread. Yesterday, we learned how to ⁶ _____ potatoes. I mean, make French fries! That was so much harder than you'd think. But I still like to ⁷ _____ best. Cooking burgers outdoors is my idea of fun. Hey, maybe when I come home I can cook for you and your friends. That would be fun!

Write back soon,

Justin

3 Answer the questions with your own information.

1. Which cooking activities from Exercise 1 are your favorites?

   I like baking cookies and cakes.

   _____

2. What is your favorite way to prepare chicken?

   _____

3. What is the easiest way to cook something?

   _____

4. What is the most difficult way to cook something?

   _____

1 Check (✓) if the sentence uses first conditional or zero conditional.

	First conditional (possible results)	Zero conditional (always true)
1. When you bake a cake, you need to measure the ingredients carefully.		✓
2. If we don't clean up after the picnic, mice will come.		
3. You don't have to add salt, unless you like really salty food.		
4. If Tom eats shrimp, he gets a rash.		
5. I don't want a slice of cake, unless you want to share one.		
6. When it's been a cold winter, the price of oranges goes up.		

2 Correct the first conditional sentences.

1. If I ~~will~~ eat a hamburger for dinner, I won't eat dessert afterward.

2. If we eat Chinese food tonight, we use chopsticks.

3. I not eat dessert at the restaurant, unless they have chocolate cake.

4. If she eats too many cookies this afternoon, her stomach hurt.

5. You want to have some of this delicious pizza, unless you don't like tomatoes.

3 Correct the zero conditional sentences.

will
1. When you boil an egg too fast, it ˄turn grey inside.

2. If you won't use enough water to boil rice, it becomes too sticky.

3. Meat won't cook through evenly when you will put it on the grill cold from the refrigerator.

4. When your stomach will hurt, you can drink some mint tea.

5. You can take away some of the bad smell if you will rinse fresh garlic under water before using it.

4 Complete the conversation. When possible, use the first conditional. If the zero conditional is needed, write X.

Ellen: Hi, Rafe. What are you cooking?

Rafe: I'm going to cook this fish. I can't decide if I want to fry it or grill it, though.

Ellen: Well, when you fry fish, the whole house ¹ _X_ smells.

Rafe: That's true. But if I open the window, it ² _____ smell.

Ellen: Well, not as much.

Rafe: If I grill the fish outside, the house ³ _____ smell.

Ellen: Yes, but the grill takes a long time to heat up. You ⁴ _____ need to heat it up now if you want to eat dinner by seven.

Rafe: Oh, I forgot about that. Do you think there's enough time?

Ellen: I'm not sure. Maybe we should just go out to dinner at the Seaside Café.

Rafe: That fancy new place?! If you want to eat at the Seaside Café, you ⁵ _____ need to make a reservation two weeks ahead of time! Besides, I can't go unless you pay. I spent all my money on the fish!

Ellen: You know, if we bake the fish in the oven, it ⁶ _____ take very long.

VOCABULARY Adjectives
describing food

1 Find nine more adjectives that describe food.

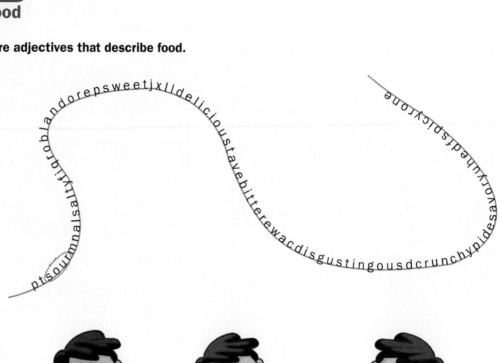

ptsourmnalsaltyfkjgroblandorepsweetjxlldelicioustavebitterewacdisgustingousdcrunchypidesavorykyhnedtspicytone

2 Circle the food or drink the first word best describes.

1. sour	a. banana	b. lemon
2. sweet	a. candy	b. French fries
3. bitter	a. milk	b. coffee
4. crunchy	a. steak	b. tortilla chips
5. salty	a. cake	b. potato chips
6. spicy	a. chili peppers	b. grapes
7. delicious	a. celery	b. pizza
8. disgusting	a. fried spiders	b. bread
9. savory	a. burgers	b. strawberries
10. bland	a. crackers	b. nachos

3 Complete the sentences. Use some of the words from Exercise 2. More than one answer may be possible.

1. John broke a tooth when he was eating
   _____*crunchy*_____ peanuts.

2. Helen's stomach hurts. She should eat some
   _____ food, like rice or toast.

3. I like to eat curry if it's not too
   _____. But sometimes the flavor
   is just too hot!

4. My sister can't cook. One time, she made chicken noodle soup and added chocolate to it. It was _____! No one could eat it.

5. My mother only drinks coffee with milk and sugar. She says it's too _____ otherwise.

6. In Japan, a lot of people say sushi is the most _____ food. That's why they serve it on special occasions.

7. I'm always thirsty after I eat in a restaurant. Restaurant food is so _____.

8. I usually eat something _____ like ham and eggs for breakfast instead of something _____ like pancakes.

9. Mom forgot to add sugar to the lemonade, and it was so _____!

4 Answer the questions. Use your own ideas.

1. What is your favorite salty food? _____

2. What is your favorite sweet food? _____

3. What two flavors do you like to combine?

   _____

4. What food do you think is disgusting?

   _____

Second conditional review

1 Complete the chart with the second conditional to describe imaginary situations and possible consequences.

Yes/No questions

1. _Would_ you order fried *chapulines* _if_ they _were_ on the menu?

No, I _wouldn't_ .

I _wouldn't_ eat them _if_ you paid me.

2. _____ someone offered them to you, _____ you eat insects?

Yes, I _____ .

No, _____ someone offered them to me, I _____ eat them.

Wh- questions

3. _____ you had to give up a favorite food, which one _____ you give up?

I _____ probably give up hamburgers.

4. What food _____ you try _____ you were in Australia?

I _____ probably try fried alligator.

2 Circle the correct answers.

Elena: Hey, Chris. ①*If* / **Would** somebody offered you fried alligator tail, **were / would** you eat it?

Chris: I probably [2]**was / would**.

Elena: Ew! Really?

Chris: Yeah. I [3]**were / would** try anything once.

Elena: OK. [4]**If / Would** you **was / were** really hungry, **if / would** you eat horse meat?

Chris: Hmm. I don't know. Oh, I probably [5]**did / would**.

Elena: OK. [6]**Did / Would** you still eat horse meat **if / were** you met the horse first?

Chris: You got me. No, [7]**if / would** I met the horse first, then I probably **weren't / wouldn't**.

3 Write second conditional questions with the information in the chart.

	Imaginary situation	Possible consequence
1.	we / be / Japan	what / we / eat
2.	you / can learn to cook / anything	what / it / be
3.	Tina / have to give up / bread or rice	which / she / give up
	Possible consequence	**Imaginary situation**
4.	Aldo / eat jellyfish	he / be alone on an island
5.	they / eat raw meat	they / have no other choice

1. _If we were in Japan, what would we eat?_

2. _____

3. _____

4. _____

5. _____

4 Write the questions another way. Then answer the questions with your own information.

1. Would you eat *fugu* if it were offered to you?

Q: _If it were offered to you, would you eat fugu?_

A: _No, I wouldn't._

2. If you were to cook a meal to impress someone, what would you cook?

Q: _____

_____

A: _____

3. If you could try any new food, what would you try?

Q: _____

A: _____

4. If you could eat as much of a food as you'd like, what would you eat?

Q: _____

_____

A: _____

1. Circle the correct answers.

1. When you use just a little bit of something, it's called **a pinch** / **a simmer**.

2. You can use a spoon to **simmer / stir** something.

3. You can **pinch / pour** something liquid, such as milk or oil.

4. When you **pour / simmer** sauce, it is not as hot as when you boil it.

5. "**First of all**"/ "**Then add**" is the phrase that comes before the step you do at the beginning.

6. If you pour some milk onto cereal, you are **adding /simmering** it to the cereal.

2 Complete the conversation with the expressions from Exercise 1.

Ernie: Hey, Jack. Would you like some breakfast? I'm going to cook some eggs.

Jack: Why don't you make an omelet?

Ernie: I've never cooked an omelet before, but I can try.

Jack: It's easy. I'll tell you how to do it. ¹*First of all*, you need to take the skin off the tomato. ²_____ it in hot water for a few minutes. Then the skin comes off easily. Then you can chop it.

Ernie: OK. Now what?

Jack: Next, you need to beat about four eggs. ³_____ the tomatoes to the eggs. I like to add some herbs and a ⁴_____ of salt and pepper. Gently ⁵_____ it with a wide spoon.

Ernie: We have parsley and chives, so I'll add those herbs.

Jack: Great. Put some oil into a pan and heat it up. When the pan is hot, ⁶_____ the egg mixture into it.

Ernie: Got it. How does this look?

Jack: Use a fork to lift the cooked edges up and let the egg liquid run underneath. That's right. And we're done!

READING TO WRITE

1 Complete the sentences with the correct words.

a great deal of	a lot of	not enough
not much	so	such
too much		

1. If you put ____too much____ water in the pot, it will spill over when it boils.

2. What did you put in this stew? It is _____ delicious!

3. This tastes bland! There are _____ herbs in it.

4. I don't think we need any more pepper in the soup. There's _____ it in the soup already.

5. Can you pass the salt, please? I like _____ salt on my French fries.

6. This is _____ good bread! You are really good at baking.

7. This is a healthy cookie recipe. There's _____ sugar in it.

2 Complete the text with some of the phrases from Exercise 1.

My Grandmother's Signature Dish

by Iris

My grandmother is from Portugal, near Spain. Every year around the holidays, she makes our family's signature dish: *Bacalhau*. It is a salted, dried cod fish that is served in many different ways, often with potatoes. People say there are 365 different ways to prepare *bacalhau* – one for each day of the year. It is ¹ _such_ a common dish in Europe and places like the Dominican Republic and Puerto Rico. The dish originated in Norway, where the cod fish is found.

To make the dish, you fry the fish in a pan with some onions and garlic. You add a pinch of salt and pepper, but not ² _____ salt! There is ³ _____ salt in the fish already.

Then you spread some oil in a pan. You put chopped potatoes, carrots, and cabbage in the bottom of the pan. Then you put the cod fish and onions and garlic on top of it. You bake it in the oven for about 30 minutes. To serve it, you put sliced boiled eggs and olives on top. It is ⁴ _____ delicious!

There are ⁵ _____ variations; some people add chickpeas (garbanzos) or cream. You should try them all!

3 Read the text again. Answer the questions.

1. What is Iris's grandmother's signature dish?

_____

2. What are the main ingredients?

_____

_____

3. How is it made?

_____

_____

4. What are some variations?

_____

_____

5. Where else is the dish eaten?

_____

_____

REVIEW UNITS 3–4

1 Write the words next to the definitions.

bake	~~end up.~~	predict
bland	fry	spicy
chop	keep on	
delicious	mix	

1. To arrive somewhere without a plan. *end up*

2. To say what will happen in the future. _____

3. To cut into small pieces or cubes. _____

4. _____ food with little flavor is the opposite of _____ food.

5. To cook something using hot oil in a pan on a stovetop. _____

6. To cook something, such as a cake or cookies, using dry heat in the oven. _____

7. To continue and not stop or give up.

_____

8. To combine different things together.

_____

9. A lively flavor that is often called "hot."

_____

2 Complete the sentences with a word from each box.

break	an award
develop	a business
do	~~the community.~~
start	a project
~~support.~~	a record
win	volunteer work

1. Sue has donated money to fund the new playground. She wants to *support the community*.

2. Ralph has been running a lot, and his time is faster than everyone's. He's probably going to _____ in the next race.

3. They plan to _____ that will bring fresh water to the area.

4. I just think that everyone should _____ _____ at some point in their life. It feels good to help people.

5. Elon says he will _____ when he graduates from school. He wants to make a lot of money.

6. Carol sold the most houses this year, so she is going to _____.

3 Look at the pictures and complete the puzzle. Then complete the sentences about Mia by unscrambling the letters in the grey boxes.

Mia will probably _____ being a chef.

across

5.   7.   8.

down

1.   2.   3.

4.  6.  7.

4 Put the words in the correct order to make sentences. Write each sentence two ways.

1. you / eat fugu / should / to take / if / you / like / risks / .

If you like to take risks, you should eat fugu.

You should eat fugu, _____

2. you / like / the jellyfish / don't / unless / order / unusual tastes / .

_____

_____

3. eat / when / your breath / you / garlic / smells / .

_____

_____

4. will be / you add / unless / a lot of / spices / this chili / bland / .

_____

_____

5. be bitter / add / if / will / you / sugar / don't / the coffee / .

_____

_____

6. a Japanese restaurant / we go / when / eat / won't / Steve / sushi / to / .

_____

_____

5 **Look at Anya's Life Plan list. Then complete the questions and answers about her plans. Use *will*, *going to*, the future continuous, and future perfect.**

> ### My Life Plan, April 2016:
>
> June 2016 — Graduate from college
>
> July 2016 — Start a website
>
> July to August 2016 — Save money from summer job
>
> September 2016 — Move to Austin, get job
>
> September 2016 — Volunteer at animal shelter
>
> January 2017 — Develop a project to help dogs

1. Where _is_ Anya _going to move_ ?

   She _is going to move to_ Austin.

2. Where _____ she _____ in September?

   She's _____ at an animal shelter.

3. _____ she _____ from her summer job by September?

   Yes, _____.

4. What _____ she _____ by July 2016?

   She _____ a website.

5. What _____ she _____ in January of 2017?

   She _____ a project to help dogs.

6 **Complete the conversations with the correct phrases.**

add	because of	since
a pinch of	~~first of all~~	so that
as a result	let it simmer	

1. **A:** How do I sign up for this volunteer program?

   B: _First of all_ , you need to fill out this application online.

2. **A:** How much sugar should I add to your coffee?

   B: Just _____ sugar, please.

3. **A:** What do I do after I've added the chicken to the soup?

   B: Turn down the heat and then _____ for at least half an hour.

4. **A:** Why isn't Mitchell making limeade for the picnic?

   B: He said limes cost too much this year _____ of the bad weather!

5. **A:** Why isn't Jeanne coming to the party this weekend?

   B: She isn't coming _____ her new job. She has to work on weekends now.

6. **A:** I'm making hot chocolate. It's almost done.

   B: _____ just a drop of vanilla at the end. It really improves the flavor.

7. **A:** Why isn't Helen eating meat?

   B: She's stopped eating it _____ she watched that documentary about farms.

8. **A:** Are you taking classes next fall?

   B: Yes, I am. I changed my schedule at work _____ I can take two classes.

5 *Fame and* **Fortune**

VOCABULARY Verbs expressing opinion

1 **Unscramble the words to make verbs to express opinions.**

1. E T H A _____ *hate* _____

2. R E D A I M _____

3. L E F E _____

4. N O M R E M D C E _____

5. P E F E R R _____

6. P E T E R C S _____

7. P E T E R C A P A I _____

8. K H I N T _____

9. K E D S I I L _____

2 **Circle the correct answers.**

1. Jack never watches horror movies. He _____ documentaries.

   a. thinks   b. (prefers)   c. hates

2. Eliza _____ action movies. She thinks most of them are about special effects and not an actual story.

   a. hates   b. recommends   c. feels

3. Although Ben dislikes singing in musicals, he _____ the talented actors who perform in them.

   a. dislikes   b. prefers   c. appreciates

4. I _____ that it is more difficult to do comedy than dramatic acting.

   a. admire   b. hate   c. think

5. I _____ watching movies before I've read the movie reviews. I like to form my own opinions.

   a. prefer   b. admire   c. respect

6. I _____ actors who do their own stunts. It's exciting to watch an actor who has learned to ride a motorcycle or jump from a building.

   a. dislike   b. feel   c. respect

7. Mary _____ famous actors, but she wouldn't want to be one.

   a. admires   b. thinks   c. prefers

8. Jim _____ people who star in reality shows only want fame.

   a. prefers   b. thinks   c. hates

3 **Unscramble the questions. Then answer the questions using the words from Exercise 1 and your own information.**

1. about / you / How / usually / documentaries / feel / do / ?

   How do you usually feel about documentaries?

   I appreciate the people who make documentaries.

   They call attention to important issues.

2. kind / prefer / do / of / movies / What / you / ?

   _____

   _____

3. celebrity / admire / the most / do / Which / you / ?

   _____

   _____

4. friends / would / to / What / recommend / movie / you / your / ?

   _____

   _____

5. dislike / do / reality TV shows / What / you / about / ?

   _____

   _____

GRAMMAR Defining and non-defining relative clauses

1 Match the defining relative clauses with their nouns. Write *who, which, that, where,* or *whose.*

Noun	Defining relative clause
1. Movies ___c___	a. _____ phones were hacked were angry.
2. The contestants _____	b. _____ I read last week was also a movie.
3. The house _____	c. ___*that*___ don't use professional actors are interesting.
4. The celebrities _____	d. _____ are on game shows must be nervous.
5. The book _____	e. _____ the movie was filmed is now a museum.

2 Rewrite the sentences. Add the non-defining relative clause in parentheses. Use *who, which, where,* or *whose,* and commas.

1. Leonardo DiCaprio donated $2 million to the marine conservation group Oceans 5. (starred in *Titanic*)

   Leonardo DiCaprio, who starred in Titanic,

   donated $2 million to the marine

   conservation group Oceans 5.

2. Mark Zuckerberg donated millions to the Newark, New Jersey, school system. (his personal wealth is over $30 billion)

   _____

   _____

3. Potcake Place is a charity in the Turks and Caicos Islands. (its goal is to rescue a breed of dog called the "potcake")

   _____

   _____

4. Brad Pitt's charity, the Make It Right Foundation, is based in New Orleans, Louisiana. (he owns a house there)

   _____

   _____

5. Malala Yousafzai donated $50,000 to schools in Gaza. (won the Nobel Peace Prize)

   _____

   _____

6. Doctors Without Borders is helping to care for sick people in Western Africa. (operates in over 70 countries)

   _____

   _____

7. Fashion blogger Tavi Gevinson starred in a Broadway play. (her online magazine for teen girls gets 3.5 million hits per month)

   _____

   _____

8. The African Library Project works to develop libraries in English-speaking countries such as Sierra Leone. (less than 25 percent of adult women are able to read there)

   _____

   _____

3 Correct the sentences. Correct punctuation, if needed.

who

1. My friend Elizabeth, ~~which~~ volunteers at the hospital, wants to be a doctor.

2. A "philanthropist" is someone whose donates money to charities and organizations to help others.

3. My cousin's band where plays really cool music got to open for Arcade Fire in 2015.

4. It seems like the companies, who have a social mission, are more successful than those who just want to make a lot of money.

5. Captain Paul Watson whose once belonged to Greenpeace founded the Sea Shepherd Conservation Society to protect marine life.

6. We went to Mavericks Beach, that the annual big wave surfing contest takes place.

VOCABULARY Adverbs of degree

1 Circle seven more adverbs of degree. Write them in order on the chart.

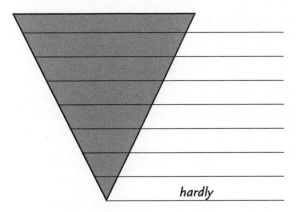

farenlyslightlyextremelyepsnearlyalgpupprettynvytyfairlyhijklyperfectlyyusoimabsolutelyzvps hardly

hardly

2 Write the words from Exercise 1 that have the same meaning.

1. very well, completely _____

_____

2. very much, really _____

3. somewhat, kind of _____,

_____

4. almost _____

5. just a little _____

6. barely at all _____

3 Put the words in the correct order to make sentences that use adverbs of degree.

1. sure / sold out / the / yet / pretty / concert / I'm / hasn't / .

I'm pretty sure the concert hasn't sold out yet.

2. about / I'm / new/ crazy / Lorde's / absolutely / album / .

_____

3. hardly / speaks / I / him / can / softly, / so / hear / Carl / .

_____

4. have / I / fairly / open / who / door / good idea / a / left / the / .

_____

5. my old one / fine / smartphone / I / don't / when / perfectly / need / works / a / new / .

_____

6. too / much / felt / eating / dinner / ill / after / slightly / for / We / .

_____

7. to / practice / become / successful / hard / extremely / Musicians / .

_____

8. nearly / Jen / was / she / fell / at / when / finish line / the / .

_____

4 Read the pairs of sentences. Rewrite the first sentence in each pair using an adverb of degree. More than one answer may be possible.

1. Haley came very close to getting a role in that new movie. But Susanne got it instead.

Haley nearly got a role in that new movie.

2. Ken sang the song the first time. He sang it exactly right!

_____

3. He would've made the goal if it had been kicked more to the right. It was very close.

_____

4. Hank looked scared during the movie. I don't think he'll ever go see another one.

_____

5. I'm convinced that I want to have a career in marine conservation. I have made my decision.

_____

GRAMMAR Tag questions

1 Match the sentences with the tag questions.

1. You watched the game last night, **b**   a. have you?

2. You were at the café yesterday, _____   b. didn't you?

3. You'd donate money if you could, _____   c. won't you?

4. You haven't been to Hollywood, _____   d. weren't you?

5. You'll clean up the kitchen, _____   e. wouldn't you?

2 Add tag questions.

1. That game was pretty close, __*wasn't it*__ ?

2. I like listening to music that makes me feel good, _____?

3. You think watching the news is boring, _____?

4. Tim almost fell asleep during the movie, _____?

5. You haven't seen Bruno Mars in concert, _____?

6. Traffic is moving extremely slowly in downtown Los Angeles, _____?

7. That's the actress who was in that movie, _____?

3 Correct the tag questions. More than one answer may be possible.

                    weren't

1. The tickets were expensive, ~~haven't~~ they?

2. This show is funny, doesn't it?

3. Kids shouldn't play video games so often, aren't they?

4. This is the way to the museum, can it?

5. They really like all of the *Star Wars* movies, should they?

6. Uma Thurman's father is a college professor, OK?

7. Bill Murray often plays jokes on ordinary people, would he?

8. Adam Levine from Maroon 5 does yoga, can't he?

4 Write questions. Use the tag questions and your own information.

1. (isn't it) __*It's Monday today, isn't it?*__

   _____

2. (haven't they)

   _____

3. (weren't we)

   _____

4. (doesn't it)

   _____

5. (right)

   _____

CONVERSATION Making a point

1. Circle the correct answers.

1. **A:** This movie is going to be boring, isn't it?

   B: _____ It might be interesting.

   a. Of course.   b. Not necessarily!

2. **A:** If everybody had to do some volunteer work, people might be nicer to each other.

   B: _____ And it might make people feel a sense of community.

   a. Not necessarily!   b. That's a good point.

3. **A:** The books are always better than the movies, right?

   B: _____ The actors are never like you picture the characters.

   a. As far as I'm   b. Of course!
   concerned.

4. **A:** Want to take some more golf lessons?

   B: _____, those are the last lessons I want to take!

   a. As far as I'm   b. You're absolutely right
   concerned

5. **A:** Do you think celebrities support charities for publicity or because they care?

   B: _____ some of them do it because they care.

   a. Not necessarily   b. It seems to me that

6. **A:** I bet I won't like some of this music 10 years from now.

   B: _____. People's taste in music can change.

   a. As far as I'm   b. You're absolutely right
   concerned

2 Circle the correct answers.

1. **Bill:** I'm excited about the sci-fi conference! Hey, are you wearing that? ¹**It seems to me that** / **Not necessarily** it would be better if we wore similar costumes.

   Ted: ²**As far as I'm concerned.** / **You're absolutely right**. That's why I got you a costume like mine!

2. **Esther:** So which movie did you like best, *The Hobbit* or *Star Wars*?

   Michelle: *The Hobbit*, ³**it seems to me** / **of course**. The original *Star Wars* just looks so dated.

   Esther: ⁴**Not necessarily.** / **That's a good point**. *The Hobbit* movie does look more modern.

3. **Alexis:** One Direction is the best boy band ever!

   Mother: ⁵**Not necessarily!** / **It seems to me!** Back in my day, we loved New Kids on the Block. ⁶**That's a good point / As far as I'm concerned**, they're the best boy band ever!

1 Number the parts of a comparison/contrast essay in order from 1–3.

_____ Give similarities and differences in two separate paragraphs.

_____ State your opinion again in a different way.

_____ State your opinion about the topic.

2 Read the sentences that compare Hollywood movies from the United States to Bollywood movies from India. Match the sentences that are about the same topics.

Hollywood

1. The United States has almost 40,000 movie theaters. _f_

2. Hollywood movies make about $51 billion each year. _____

3. A single Hollywood film targets a specific genre, such as action, or sci-fi. _____

4. Hollywood makes excellent action, sci-fi, and spy movies. _____

5. In 2013, Hollywood produced over 600 films. _____

6. An average Hollywood movie costs about $47.7 million to make.

Bollywood

a. A single Bollywood film includes a lot of variety: musical numbers, action, comedy, and romance.

b. Bollywood produces about 1,000 films each year.

c. Bollywood movies make over $3 billion each year.

d. A Bollywood movie costs about $1.5 million to make.

e. Bollywood makes wonderful musicals with great song lyrics.

f. There are fewer than 13,000 movie theaters in India.

3 Combine the matching sentences from Activity 2 using the _as . . . as_ phrases.

almost twice as many . . . as	nearly as much . . . as
~~as much . . . as~~	not as many . . . as
just as . . . as	nowhere near as . . . as

1. Hollywood movies don't have __as much__ variety __as__ Bollywood movies.

2. Bollywood movies are _____ expensive to make _____ Hollywood movies.

3. There are _____ movie theaters in India _____ in the United States.

4. Bollywood films are _____ good _____ Hollywood films.

5. Bollywood films don't make _____ money _____ Hollywood movies.

6. Bollywood produces _____ films _____ Hollywood per year.

6 It's the Little Things.

VOCABULARY Everyday objects

1 Match the sentences with the pictures.

1.
   e

2.
   ___

3.
   ___

4.
   ___

5.
   ___

6.
   ___

7.
   ___

8.
   ___

9.
   ___

10.
    ___

a. I can't find the remote control for the television!

b. Don't forget to put out the candles.

c. Do you have a spare phone charger?

d. It's hot in here! Turn on the fan, please.

e. Can you turn on the light? The switch is over there.

f. I'm a bit chilly. Let's turn off the air conditioner.

g. Have you seen the matches?

h. When I traveled to London, I couldn't use my hairdryer! The plug was different!

i. Don't forget to turn off that heater before you go to bed.

j. The stores only sell those new light bulbs that save energy.

2 Read the situations and circle the correct answers.

1. Jan is driving in her car. It is cold. What should she turn on?

   a. the charger   b. the fan   c. the heater

2. The power goes out in Ha Jin's apartment at night. What can he use for light?

   a. a candle   b. a light bulb   c. a switch

3. Tracy is camping. She has gathered logs. What does she need to start a fire?

   a. a fan   b. matches   c. a remote control

4. Now the power is on in Ha Jin's apartment. What does he need to press to turn on the light?

   a. a heater   b. a plug   c. a switch

5. Now the lamp in Ha Jin's apartment doesn't work. What does he need to replace?

   a. the air conditioner   b. the light bulb   c. the remote control

6. Jan is driving in her car, and now it is very hot. What should she turn on?

   a. the air conditioner   b. the light bulb   c. matches

7. Tracy's cell phone won't turn on. What does she probably need to make it work?

   a. a charger   b. a heater   c. a switch

8. At night, the air is very still and it is hot in Jan's hotel room. What does she turn on?

   a. a candle   b. a fan   c. a heater

9. The switch for the fan in Jan's hotel room doesn't work. What should she check?

   a. the charger   b. the light bulb   c. the plug

10. Tracy wants to watch a movie. What does she use to turn on the TV?

    a. an air condiioner   b. a plug   c. a remote control

3 Answer the questions with the words from Exercise 1 and your own information.

1. When does your family use candles?

   We use candles for birthdays and special

   dinners.

   _____

   _____

2. Which months of the year do you use a heater?

   _____

   _____

3. Which months of the year do you use a fan or an air conditioner?

   _____

   _____

4. Which two items from Exercise 1 do you use the most? For what?

   _____

   _____

GRAMMAR Passive infinitive

1 Complete the chart using the passive infinitive.

	Present	Past
1. want/know	Raul *wants to be known* for his popularity.	Raul *wanted to be known* for his singing ability.
2. have/ charge	Lara's phone _____ every few hours.	Lara's phone _____ overnight.
3. like/laugh at	The comedian _____ when he's funny.	The comedian *didn't* _____ when he made the mistake.
4. expect/ treat	We _____ fairly in school.	We _____ fairly at summer camp.
5. not have/ pay	The full price _____ by students.	The full price _____ when the students went to the theater.
6. not need/ see	This movie _____ by anyone over the age of five.	This movie _____ in 3-D.

2 Complete the paragraph with the present and past passive infinitive forms of the verbs.

Our new apartment in Miami was a mess when we moved in! We ¹*didn't expect it to be messed up* (not expect it / mess up) because it was clean when we first saw it.

The air conditioner was really dusty. It ² _____ (need / clean) right away because it was hot when we moved in. It works now, which is good. The plugs on one wall didn't work either. We had to put the sofa and table, things that ³ _____ (not have / plug in), against that wall. They still need to be fixed. And all of the light bulbs ⁴ _____ (have / replace) as soon as we find the time to do it.

At least the carpet ⁵ _____ (not have / clean) when we moved in. The heater is broken, but it ⁶ _____ (not need / fix) right away. It's so hot here right now, we don't expect to use it for months!

Passive with modals

3 Rewrite the present sentences from Exercise 1 as modals. Use *must, should, might*, or *had better*. More than one answer may be possible.

1. Raul *wants to be* known for his popularity. >

   Raul must be known for his popularity.

2. _____

3. _____

4. _____

5. _____

6. _____

4 Complete the sentences using your own ideas. Use the passive infinitive or modals.

1. My smartphone needs *to be turned off at school* .

   My smartphone needs _____ .

2. His new laptop might _____ .

3. The candle has _____ .

4. The matches must _____ .

5. We didn't expect _____ .

1 Circle seven more modifiers. Then write them in the chart.

masobf**notreally**ndpalt**extremely**jaz**fartoo**bicnewt**otally**sigmr**idiculously**plutroa**kindof**enly**alittlebit**ood

1. ___ ___ ___ ___ ___ ___ ___ ___ ___ ___ ___ ___
2. ___ ___ ___ ___ ___ ___ ___ ___ ___
3. ___ ___ ___   ___ ___ ___ ___
4. _s_ _o_
5. ___ ___ ___ ___ ___ ___ ___
6. ___ ___ ___ ___   ___ ___ ___
7. ___ ___   ___ ___ ___ ___ ___ ___ ___   ___ ___ ___ ___
8. ___ ___ ___   ___ ___ ___ ___ ___ ___ ___

2 Look at the pictures. Circle the correct answers.

1. My bike is **not really / ridiculously** small. I don't think I can ride it anymore.

2. Let's turn off the air conditioner. It's **a little bit / far too** chilly in here! My hands are freezing!

3. I want a new laptop, but this one's **not really / so** expensive. I don't have enough money to buy it.

4. That dress is **kind of / far too** nice to wear while you paint your room!

5. That watch is **kind of / not really** cool. But I don't think it has enough features.

6. My grandmother thinks it's **extremely / not really** important to have a smartphone. She still doesn't have one.

7. That car is **a little bit / so** cool! It's the most amazing car I've ever seen!

8. Personally, I'm **not really / totally** bored with that social networking site. I'm going to quit visiting it.

3 Complete the sentences with a word or phrase from each box and your own ideas.

extremely	colorful
far too	cool
a little bit	dangerous
kind of	difficult
not really	easy
ridiculously	expensive
so	old
totally	small

1. *My brother's smartphone is far too old to*

   take videos.

2. _____

3. _____

4. _____

5. _____

6. _____

7. _____

8. _____

GRAMMAR Review of causative *have/get*

1 Match the active sentences with the passive/causative sentences.

Active	Passive/Causative
1. Someone repairs her bike after a race. **b**	a. She isn't having her bike repaired after the race.
2. Someone repaired her bike after the race. ___	b. She has her bike repaired after a race.
3. No one is repairing her bike after the race. ___	c. She'll get her bike repaired after the race.
4. She'll ask someone to repair her bike after the race. ___	d. Must she have her bike repaired after the race?
5. Must she get someone to repair her bike after the race? ___	e. She got her bike repaired after the race.

2 Put the words in the correct order to make sentences.

1. his charger / got / fixed / last night / Andrew / .

   Andrew got his charger fixed last night.

2. to do / for me / get / I / can never / my brother / my homework / .

   _____

3. I / cut / the / have / lawn / Should / you / for / ?

   _____

4. camera / isn't / his / boy / The / checked / getting / today / .

   _____

5. weekend / get / school / painted / The / won't / this /.

   _____

6. cleaned / on / have / team uniforms / We / our / weekends /.

   _____

3 Rewrite the sentences. Use the tense and voice (active or causative) in parentheses.

1. Someone <u>paints</u> Mike's skateboard on Friday. (simple past/active)

   Someone *painted Mike's skateboard on Friday.*

2. I <u>will fix</u> my laptop this weekend. (future with *will*/causative)
   I will _____

3. Someone <u>cuts</u> Tom's hair every three months. (simple present/passive)
   Tom _____

4. The man <u>isn't having anyone set up</u> his website. (present continuous/active) No one
   _____ the man's website.

5. Someone professionally <u>photographed</u> Elizabeth's birthday party. (simple past/causative)
   Elizabeth _____

1 Put the words in the correct order to complete the phrase. Match the phrases to the second part of questions 1–6.

> you / could / show /
> it / does / have /
> model / is / which /
> it / to / is / easy / use /
> is / how / good / it /
> does / how / it / long /

1. _Could you show_ us how to use the video function?

2. _____ last before you have to charge it?

3. _____ the newest?

4. _____ compared to the previous version?

5. _____ or do I need to read the instructions?

6. _____ any extra batteries?

2 Complete the conversation with the phrases from Exercise 1.

Hiroki: Excuse me. ¹ _Could you show_ me this digital camera?

Salesperson: Here you are.

Hiroki: Thank you.

Emma: Hiroki, that one's OK. But ² _____ to use in the water? I don't think that kind is waterproof.

Hiroki: Oh, you're right. But ³ _____?

Emma: Yeah, it's really easy because it's totally basic. But look, it says it's not waterproof.

Emma (to salesperson): Excuse me, ⁴ _____ the waterproof one?

Salesperson: This one is.

Emma: ⁵ _____ take to charge?

Salesperson: About two hours.

Emma: See, Hiroki? That's pretty fast.

Hiroki: ⁶ _____ GPS?

Salesperson: Of course, it does.

Emma: Oh, gosh. Look at the price!

Hiroki: Wow, that's expensive!

READING TO WRITE

1 Combine the underlined sentences with *while* or *whereas*. Make any other changes necessary.

Bass Boss Headphones v2

posted by Josephine

This review is for Bass Boss Headphones v2. I found them on sale online for $89.99. ¹That seems ridiculously expensive for a pair of headphones. It's about ten dollars less than the older version and about ten times better!

First of all, the new v2 model headphones sound *amazing*. ²The v1 headphones sound good. These sound great. Your ears will enjoy cleaner high notes, deeper bass notes, and an overall crisp sound. And they have excellent sound-elimination technology!

³I liked using the old headphones on may way to school. I love the new ones even more. I can hear every note even when I'm on a noisy bus! They're also useful for studying languages. I plug mine in to my laptop when I study English.

⁴The v1 had a good design. These fit better. ⁵The v2 model looks sleeker. The previous version was kind of clunky. ⁶The v1 model only came in black or white. This new model comes in 20 fun colors, like orange or green. The new version is lighter, too!

Finally, there's a new feature for v2. You can press a button on the cord to mute the sound so you can hear what's going on around you. Perfect for when your mom's calling you to come to dinner.

I think these are great headphones. They have more useful features than the previous version. I recommend buying them on sale.

1. *While that seems ridiculously expensive for a pair of headphones, it's about ten dollars less than the older version and about ten times better!*
2. _____
3. _____
4. _____
5. _____
6. _____

2 Read the article in Exercise 1 again. Circle the correct answers.

1. What does Josephine say about the price of the Bass Boss Headphones v2?

   a. She says it was ten dollars.

   b. She says they weren't on sale.

   c. She says they cost a lot.

2. What is different about the v2 model headphones?

   a. They're lighter, and they sound better, fit better, and come in more colors.

   b. They're ridiculously expensive, kind of clunky, and noisy.

   c. They only come in orange or green.

3. What are they useful for?

   a. for recording sounds

   b. for listening to music and studying

   c. for hearing your mother call you

4. What new feature does the v2 model have?

   a. It can be plugged into a laptop.

   b. It can be found on sale.

   c. The sound can be muted.

5. What is her recommendation?

   a. not to buy it

   b. to buy it on sale

   c. to buy the v1 headphones

1 Circle the correct answers.

1. This plug looks **a little bit** / **ridiculously** bent. I think it needs to be replaced.

2. I **dislike** / **feel** the position of this switch. It's difficult to reach.

3. This remote control is **absolutely** / **hardly** amazing! It can turn on **fairly** / **nearly** everything in this room!

4. Can we turn off the air conditioner now? I **appreciate** / **think** the room is cool enough.

5. I **recommend** / **respect** these light bulbs for your art studio. They are nice and bright.

6. I **admire** / **recommend** that you get a new phone charger. This one works **not really** / **so** slowly!

7. I **hate** / **respect** this fan. It's **far too** / **not really** noisy!

8. I'm **pretty** / **ridiculously** satisfied with this heater. It works **hardly** / **perfectly** fine, even though it was inexpensive.

2 Match the sentences from Exercise 1 with the pictures.

a. ___1___   b. _____

c. _____   d. _____

e. _____   f. _____

g. _____   h. _____

3 Cross out the word that doesn't belong in each category.

1. Expressing an opinion:

   feel   hate   respect   ridiculously

2. Everyday objects:

   a little bit   a fan   a plug   a switch

3. Words that modify others:

   extremely   far too   kind of   remote control

4. Adverbs that show degree:

   hardly   nearly   pricey   pretty

4 Put the words in the correct order to make sentences.

1. my grandfather / I / cleaned / the yard / for / get / will / .

   I will get the yard cleaned for my grandfather.

2. it / fixed / for / have / I / you / Should / ?

   _____

3. the car / cleaned / got / Friday / on / They / .

   _____

4. of / blog posts / get / people / Her / read / by / a lot / .

   _____

5. delivered / aren't / a pizza / Our friends / house / to / their / having /.

   _____

6. her / Kim / mother's / have / replaced / air conditioner / will / .

   _____

5 Rewrite the sentences. Change the verbs from active to passive.

1. People know Maya for her beautiful voice.

   Maya is known for her beautiful voice.

2. Nobody needed to turn the air conditioner on.

   _____

3. Someone put out the candles before bedtime.

   _____

4. People know Terry for his inventions, and he likes that.

   _____

5. We turned our phones off during class, which Mrs. Cook expected.

   _____

6 Complete the conversations with tag questions.

1. **A:** You still listen to Katy Perry, _don't you_ ?

   B: Not as much as I used to.

2. **A:** You've already seen *Guardians of the Galaxy*, _____ ?

   B: A long time ago.

3. **A:** You're buying the latest smartphone, _____ ?

   B: Not right away.

4. **A:** That was an exciting game last night, _____ ?

   B: I'll say! I was on the edge of my seat!

5. **A:** Sports stars should make less money, _____ ?

   B: I guess so. But the really good ones sell a lot of tickets.

6. **A:** Rap music is getting kind of old, _____ ?

   B: Kind of. I like it, but I just don't listen to it as much as I used to.

7 Combine the sentences using defining or non-defining relative clauses. More than one answer may be correct.

1. I think people are desperate for attention. They go on reality TV shows.

   I think people who are desperate for attention
   go on reality TV shows.

2. My friend Rebecca was on a reality TV show. She's an interior designer.

   _____

   _____

3. Rebecca was starting a design business. Starting a design business is hard to do.

   _____

   _____

4. She got on a reality show. The reality show redecorates people's homes.

   _____

   _____

5. They redecorated for people. The people's homes had been ruined in a flood.

   _____

   _____

8 Complete the conversation.

~~Could you show me~~	It seems to me that
Does it have	That's a good point.
How good is	Which model

Sophia: Hey, Noah. [1] *Could you show me* your tablet?

Noah: Sure. Are you thinking about buying one?

Sophia: Yeah. [2]_____ a video camera?

Noah: Yes, it does.

Sophia: [3]_____ the video quality, though? I need to use it for my video class assignments.

Noah: It's pretty good.

Sophia: [4]_____ has the best quality camera?

Noah: Oh, not this one. [5]_____ you'd be happier with the upgraded version. But it's more expensive.

Julia: Yeah, but if I can take better videos, that will help me get a better grade in class, right?

Noah: Oh, well, yeah. [6]_____

7 Have a Ball!

1 Unscramble the words to make celebration phrases. Then number the pictures.

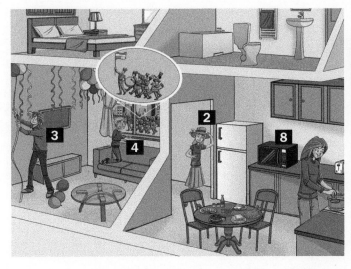

1. A L P Y   C S U M I   *play music*
2. S R E S D   P U
3. T U P   P U   R E D O O N S I A C T
4. C H A W T   A   A D E R P A
5. E V H A   A   D O O G   M I T E

6. V E G I A   T R E E N P S
7. E S T   F O F   R O R K I W E S F
8. P E A R R E P   L I S P A C E   O D O F
9. D L H O   A   S T O N E C T

2 Circle the correct answers.

1. Our neighbor **has a good time / puts up decorations** for nearly every holiday. People from all over town drive by his house to see them.

2. My favorite part of celebrating is when people **give a present / set off fireworks**. They look so pretty in the night sky.

3. My grandfather won't go with us anymore to **prepare special foods / watch the parade**. He said he doesn't like crowds.

4. Tino comes to every party. He really likes to **have a good time / hold a contest**.

5. Bridget likes to **dress up / play music** at parties, but she'll let you suggest songs.

6. I love costume parties! Especially when they **hold a contest / prepare special food**. I usually have creative ideas and win.

7. My boyfriend doesn't like going to weddings because he doesn't like to **dress up / watch a parade**.

8. My family always **plays music / prepares special food** for our celebrations. We've been making the same delicious dishes for years!

9. My brother likes to **give presents / hold contests**. He makes all his gifts by hand.

1 Circle the correct answers. If both answers are possible, circle both.

1. Tiffany hates **going / to go** to parties.

2. Michael learned **dancing / to dance** for his wedding.

3. They're considering **having / to have** a New Year's party.

4. We haven't forgotten **bringing / to bring** a dish to the party.

5. My uncle started **grilling / to grill** the chicken already.

6. My younger sister tried **staying up/ to stay up** until midnight on New Year's Eve, but she fell asleep at 11 o'clock.

2 Correct the sentences with either the infinitive or *-ing* form. If the sentences are already correct, write *correct*.

1. What kind of music do you want ~~playing~~ at the party? _____
   to play

2. Do you remember to go a concert for the first time? _____

3. Some people don't like to dress up in costumes. _____

4. My sister doesn't enjoy to eat cake on her birthday. _____

5. My cousin plans having her graduation party at home. _____

6. Don't forget cleaning the house before the party. _____

7. Rachel and Tom discussed to have their wedding in Sonoma. _____

8. Heather loves to sing karaoke at parties. _____

3 Put the words in the correct order to make sentences. When necessary, change the verbs to the infinitive or the *-ing* form. More than one answer may be possible.

1. I / can't / a / was / remember / when / have / two / birthday party / I / .

   I can't remember having a birthday party
   when I was two.

2. Tracy / arrive / at / on time / our house / expects / .

   _____

3. try / the / eat / once / at / all / Don't / candy /.

   _____

4. The / the / start / teacher / game / party / prefers / with / a / .

   _____

5. Elliot / have / his / clowns / birthday / doesn't / party / at / enjoy / .

   _____

6. celebration / get / The / noisy / after / began / the / first fireworks / .

   _____

4 Write sentences that are true for you. Use the phrases *(not) enjoy, (not) want, love, hate,* and *(not) forget* with the infinitive or the *-ing* forms of the verbs.

1. ride a bike

   I love riding a bike.

2. dress up

   _____

3. give a present

   _____

4. prepare special food

   _____

5. put up decorations

   _____

6. set off fireworks

   _____

VOCABULARY Descriptive adjectives

1 Circle nine more adjectives.

A	I	M	P	R	E	S	S	I	V	E	L
N	W	S	K	R	T	S	C	A	R	Y	I
I	E	T	S	Q	I	N	O	I	S	Y	V
A	Q	M	E	S	S	Y	V	H	R	E	E
T	R	A	D	I	T	I	O	N	A	L	L
H	Z	S	T	U	N	N	I	N	G	W	Y
P	E	A	C	E	F	U	L	V	W	A	N
L	A	V	P	J	P	Y	H	N	I	C	Q
A	W	M	G	C	R	O	W	D	E	D	H
S	Q	N	P	O	Q	H	T	K	O	E	S
E	Y	X	J	R	F	S	M	Z	C	J	Y
J	X	J	D	C	O	L	O	R	F	U	L

2 Circle the correct answers.

1. Yumi told me about the Japanese festival of *hanami*, or flower viewing. People have a picnic under the cherry blossoms in the spring. She said the women often wear a *kimono* during the *hanami* festival. A *kimono* is a kind of **crowded / lively / traditional** Japanese robe. *Hanami* sounded like a lovely, **crowded / noisy / peaceful** nature festival. But Yumi told me it was very **lively / stunning / traditional**, with lots of people singing and dancing.

2. On New Year's Eve, everyone in our city gathers downtown to wait for midnight. There are so many people! It's very **colorful / crowded / traditional**, but it feels safe and fun. When the clock strikes midnight, everyone cheers and it gets quite **colorful / messy / noisy**. My favorite part of New Year's is when the city sets off the fireworks. This year's fireworks display was particularly **peaceful / crowded / stunning**! I loved it. My younger brother didn't like the fireworks, though. He thought they were loud and **impressive / peaceful / scary**.

3. Ed went to a festival in India where people throw bright powder on each other. His photos are amazing. He has some beautiful shots of colored powder flying through the air. The powder is so **colorful / peaceful / traditional.** And it's **colorful / impressive / peaceful** that he didn't get powder all over his camera! He said the festival was wonderful, but it was very **crowded / messy / noisy**. He hasn't been able to wash the powder out of some of his clothing.

3 Write a paragraph describing a celebration, festival, or party using the words from Exercise 1 and your own information.

We celebrated my grandparent's 40th anniversary
recently. The dancing at their party was surprisingly
lively! My uncle led off with a traditional song . . .

_____

_____

_____

_____

_____

_____

_____

GRAMMAR *-ing* form (gerund) as subject; *by/for* + *-ing* form

1 How is the *-ing* form used? Read the sentences and check (✓) the correct columns.

	As the subject	To show how to do something	To show the purpose or use of something
1. **Decorating** the house for parties is my favorite part of the holidays.	✓		
2. The annual parade is an occasion for **wearing** silly hats.			
3. Not **bringing** a gift to the party would be rude.			
4. **Watching** the fireworks by the river is stunning.			
5. We began the ceremony by **singing** a song.			
6. The rainy weather isn't good for **watching** the parade.			

2 Correct the mistakes.

1. The park is perfect ~~by have~~ *for having* a picnic.

2. They celebrated their anniversary for take a long cruise.

3. One of Carrie's favorite things is for watches the leaves change color in the fall.

4. He improved his test scores to study every day.

5. My grandmother's kitchen is perfect by prepares food.

6. I tell everyone that for go to the Art Festival was the highlight of my trip.

3 Complete the conversation with the gerund forms of the verbs in parentheses. Add *by* or *for*, if necessary.

Maria: What was that festival you went to in December?

Kevin: I went to the Chocolate Festival. It's the perfect festival ¹ *for learning* (learn) about different types of chocolate.

Maria: That must be helpful since you're in culinary school, right? ² _____ (go) to the festival, you're learning something new. It's like studying for you!

Kevin: It really is. You get a sense of the variety of chocolate ³ _____ (taste) a lot of different kinds.

Maria: Oh, yeah! ⁴ _____ (no eat) as many kinds as you can would be a mistake!

Kevin: And the festival is not just about flavor. ⁵ _____ (watch) how chocolates are made is important, too.

Maria: I've heard that ⁶ _____ (make) chocolates is difficult.

Kevin: It is. ⁷ _____ (take) photos of the demonstrations has been a great way to take notes on the process.

Maria: Well, I can't wait to see what you've learned!

4 Write two sentences for each gerund phrase: one using *by* and one using *for*. Use your own ideas.

1. watch a concert

   by: *I started my weekend by watching a concert on TV.*

   for: *The outdoor theater in the park is great for watching a concert.*

   by: _____

   for: _____

2. play music

   by: _____

   for: _____

3. have a party

   by: _____

   for: _____

4. go to a festival

   by: _____

   for: _____

CONVERSATION Exclamations

1. Complete the conversation.

Great idea!	That'd be
How	That's such an
is so	~~What a~~

Josh: Hi, Lynn. I'm planning a birthday party for Glenn. I don't know what to do!

Lynn: ¹____*What a*____ nice thing to do! I'll help you. Does he know about the party or is it a surprise party?

Josh: Hey! A surprise party! ²_____ Let's do that.

Lynn: Why don't we have it at your place? That way it can be a surprise.

Josh: ³_____ smart of you to think of that! But I'm not sure about keeping it a surprise.

Lynn: Here's what you do: You pick him up to take him out for his birthday. Then you pretend to forget something at your house. Invite him in for a minute when you go back to get it. When he comes in, surprise!

Josh: ⁴_____ perfect! OK. What else do we need to do?

Lynn: He ⁵_____ into music. We'll need to make a really good playlist.

Josh: Very true. I can do that. Do we need to prepare food?

Lynn: Of course, and we'll need a cake.

Josh: Right! The cake! I almost forgot! ⁶_____ important part of a birthday!

Lynn: Totally. Oh, I have a great idea! We can get one of those cakes with a photograph on it, done in frosting!

Josh: He'd like that.

2 Circle the correct answers.

1. **A:** I think for our school dance this winter, we should get an ice sculpture!

   B: (**Great idea!**)/ **That'd be difficult.** But won't it be expensive?

2. **A:** Let's take Mike to a concert instead of throwing him a party.

   B: **How / What a** great idea! It'll feel like a huge party.

3. **A:** Melanie's favorite color is green. We can serve all green foods and drinks at the party!

   B: **How / Is so** cool! Oh, as long as it's not all vegetables!

4. **A:** Instead of having music at the party, I thought we'd sing karaoke.

   B: **That'd be / Is so** a good idea, except that Chris doesn't like singing!

5. **A:** What can I do to help with the class trip?

   B: Well, the trip **how / is so** expensive. We need to come up with ideas to raise money for it.

6. **A:** We're renting go-karts for Belinda's birthday next month!

   B: **How / That's such** a fun idea.

READING TO WRITE

1 Jennifer started a company that plans parties. Complete Jennifer's email to her friend Craig. Write *so* or *too*.

○○○

📄 📁 ✈ 📎 🗑

To CraigD@cup.net

From JenniferLee@email.net

Subject Too Fun!

Dear Craig,

I'm ¹ <u>*so*</u> excited to tell you about how my party-planning company, Too Fun!, is doing. As you know, I started by planning my high school's graduation party. A lot of people think planning a party is a lot of work, but I don't. I love it. I like it when I have so much to do that I'm almost ² _____ busy to get it all done. We held the graduation in the school auditorium. We had an old-fashioned carnival theme, with games, prizes, and fun foods that people used to eat a long time ago. People took photos and had a great time.

Next, I planned my cousin's wedding reception. She paid me for it. It was ³ _____ luxurious! I rented a gorgeous inn along the coast. It was ⁴ _____ stunning. I hired a chef to prepare all of the couple's favorite foods. I planned for ⁵ _____ much food, though! We had a lot left over. But my cousin wasn't mad that I spent ⁶ _____ much on food. She was ⁷ _____ happy about her special day to care.

The next party I'm planning is a birthday party for our neighbor's daughter. I think I'm going to rent a pony! The pictures are going to be ⁸ _____ cute! I can just imagine it now.

How are things with you? Got any plans for your college graduation party? Let me know if you need any help!

Take care,

Jennifer

---

2 Read the email in Exercise 1 again. Answer the questions.

1. What two events did Jennifer plan?

   Event 1: <u>*her high school's graduation party*</u>

   Event 2: _____ .

2. Where was each party held?

   Party 1: _____

   Party 2: _____

3. What did Jennifer have at each party?

   Party 1: _____

   Party 2: _____

4. What happened at each party?

   Party 1: _____

   Party 2: _____

5. What party is Jennifer planning next?

   _____

6. What will be special about the next party?

   _____

8 Mysteries and Secrets

1 Complete the puzzle.

(crossword puzzle grid)

Across

1. Something that you don't know is going to happen is _____.

3. Something that doesn't seem true is _____.

4. Something that doesn't happen most of the time is _____.

5. If you don't find an answer to a problem or mystery, it is _____.

6. Something that isn't recognized by most people is _____.

7. When bad things happen to you a lot, you are _____.

Down

1. Something that is not valuable or useful is _____.

2. Something that isn't needed is _____.

4. When something probably won't happen it is _____.

2 Complete the sentences with some of the words from Exercise 1. More than one answer may be correct.

1. Mysterious crop circles appeared in the farmer's field. People came up with some pretty _____ explanations, like aliens caused the circles. But it turns out they were caused by an insect that makes an _____ pattern in the ground.

2. My brother is afraid he'll get bitten by a shark even though it's very _____. Very few people get bitten, so I think worrying about it is _____.

3. What happened to pilot Amelia Earhart is still an _____ mystery. But someone may have found a piece of her plane.

4. The reporter said that Banksy is a famous graffiti artist, but his real name and identity are _____. The reporter tried to discover the artist's true identity, but was _____ in his efforts to learn the truth.

5. A detective has to be careful when she looks for clues. A fingerprint or piece of hair that might seem small and _____ could turn out to be a big clue. And sometimes clues are found in _____ places, like on the backs of paintings or in the refrigerator!

3 Answer the questions with your own information.

1. Describe a time you felt unlucky.

_____

_____

2. Describe a time something unexpected happened to you or someone you know.

_____

3. Describe something that you think is unbelievable.

_____

4. Describe something that you think is unlikely to happen to you.

_____

GRAMMAR Time clauses; present participle clauses

1 Use the chart to write sentences. Use the correct forms of the verbs. More than one answer may be possible.

Time clause	First event	Second event
1. before	Ben graduated.	He became a firefighter.
2. after	We had lived in the city for years.	We discovered our favorite restaurant.
3. when	They scored the final goal.	Helen arrived at the game.
4. when	I have enough money.	I will visit the Great Wall of China
5. before	It got dark out.	The fireworks started.

1. *Ben graduated before he became a firefighter.*

2. _____

3. _____

4. _____

5. _____

2 Complete the sentences about each pair of pictures with the correct time clauses. More than one answer may be possible.

1. She put on her helmet _before_ she went skateboarding.

2. Tina started taking photos _____ she got off the bus.

3. We saw dolphins in the river _____ our boat first left Iquitos, Peru.

4 We weren't scared _____ the bats came flying out of the cave!

3 Circle the correct answers.

1. Anna loved sushi **as soon as** / **until** she tried it.

2. José had booked his ticket to New Orleans **before** / **until** the hurricane hit. So he had to change his flight.

3. They will continue the space flight program **after** / **while** they have solved the problem.

4. Logan doesn't want to be in Chiang Mai **before** / **while** it's typhoon season.

5. The butterflies were arriving **after** / **when** the film crew was in Mexico, so they got great videos.

6. I had sore feet **before** / **after** I got my new running shoes. They are so much better than my old ones!

4 Write sentences that are true for you using time clauses. Use the words given.

1. since

   I've been interested in sharks since I was five.

   _____

2. before

   _____

3. when

   _____

4. after

   _____

VOCABULARY Reporting verbs

1 Circle the word that best replaces the underlined words.

1. Terry <u>told me</u> that there would be a surprise test on Tuesday. She did not explain how she knew that.

   a. agreed   b. claimed   c. recommended

2. By the way, when I spoke with him, Aaron <u>said</u> that he'd be studying at the library tonight.

   a. wrote   b. mentioned   c. insisted

3. My aunt finally <u>answered</u> my email asking about our family's history.

   a. replied to

   b. recommended to

   c. decided on

4. Charlotte <u>liked</u> my plan to start a book club. We're going to do it!

   a. recommended to

   b. admitted to

   c. agreed on

5. I wanted Chinese food and my sister wanted sushi, but my father <u>said</u> that we were going to get pizza for dinner.

   a. admitted   b. replied   c. decided

6. My friend <u>told me to read</u> Stephen King's novels. She thinks I'd like them.

   a. wrote   b. agreed   c. recommended

7. I knew my little brother drew on the wall, even though he wouldn't <u>say that he did</u>.

   a. admit it   b. recommend it   c. decide it

8. My mom <u>said</u> that I should clean the garage before watching TV.

   a. replied   b. claimed   c. insisted

9. The reporter <u>said in the article</u> that the mystery was solved. But the police chief didn't agree.

   a. admitted   b. agreed   c. wrote

2 Complete the sentences with the correct forms of the verbs.

admit	decide	recommend
agree	insist	reply
claim	~~mention~~	write

Alex: Hey, Bill. What's the matter?

Bill: What? Nothing! Did Haley [1] _____mention_____ something to you? She sent you over here, didn't she?

Alex: OK. I'll [2] _____ it! She [3] _____ that I find out what you're going to do.

Bill: I knew it! She [4] _____ she doesn't mind if I run for student council against her. But I know she does mind.

Alex: I think you're right. It's just, she's upset because you [5] _____ to run without talking to her first. It's weird to run against a close friend.

Bill: You know, I [6] _____ it seems that way. I really do.

Alex: Well then, why did you do it?

Bill: Mr. Wells, my Political Science teacher, said it would help my college applications. He [7] _____ that I do some extracurricular activities in school, like student council.

Alex: So, you'd ruin a friendship because you want a teacher to [8] _____ a recommendation for you?

Bill: I hadn't really thought of it that way. But then again, if Haley is a good friend, she should understand. And, if she wants to work in politics, well, she'll have to get used to some friendly competition.

Alex: So, what should I tell her?

Bill: You don't have to talk to her about it. I'll [9] _____ to her in person.

3 Answer the questions using your own information.

1. Explain something important that you decided recently.

   _____

2. What is something your parents insist that you do?

   _____

3. What book, movie, or TV show do you recommend to people the most?

   _____

1 Match the quoted speech to the reported speech.

1. She said, "Yes, I hid it in the garage."

2. He said, "I heard a strange sound around midnight."

3. He said, "Go look in the attic."

4. She asked, "Did you see anything odd?"

5. She said, "We have to leave the light on at night."

6. He said, "I was at home the entire evening."

a. He said that he was at home the entire evening.

b. She asked me if I saw anything odd.

c. She admitted to hiding it in the garage.

d. He claimed to hear a strange sound around midnight.

e. He told me to look in the attic.

f. She insisted on leaving the light on at night.

2 Change the direct speech to reported speech. Use the subjects and verb forms in parentheses.

1. "Hide the new puppy in Damian's room." (Mom / say)

   Mom said to hide the new puppy in
   Damian's room.

2. "Pretend you didn't see anything." (she / recommend)

   _____

3. "We'll meet at the old clock." (we / agree)

   _____

4. "Where were you on the night of January 7?" (he / ask)

   _____

5. "Tim is hiding under the bed." (she / admit)

   _____

6. "I know who did it." (he / insist on)

   _____

Indirect questions

3 Read the indirect questions. Write the direct questions.

1. I wonder where the treasure is hidden.

   "Where is the treasure hidden?"

2. I don't know why he recommended telling her the secret.

   _____

3. Can you tell me why he said not to tell anyone?

   _____

4. I wonder if she asked why he did it.

   _____

4 Read the conversation. Rewrite the police officer's questions as indirect questions. Then rewrite the detective's answers as reported speech. Use the words in parentheses.

Detective: What was she doing when her bag was stolen?

Police officer: She was eating lunch.

Detective: Did she see anyone take it?

Police officer: No, she didn't.

Detective: Where was her bag sitting?

Police officer: It was hanging on the back of her chair.

1. **Detective:** _Can you tell me what she was doing_
   when her bag was stolen?

2. **Police officer:** _____ (said)

3. **Detective:** _____ (wonder)

4. **Police officer:** _____ (claimed)

5. **Detective:** _____ (tell)

6. **Police officer:** _____ (mention)

CONVERSATION Confirming and denying

1. Put the words in the correct order to make sentences.

1. **A:** / is / invention / say / Richard Branson / that / people / interested in / Some / buying / your / !

   Some people say that Richard Branson is interested in buying your invention!

   B: absolutely / Yes, / !

   _____

3. **A:** / you / Is / were / attacked / true / by / a / it /shark / that / ?

   _____

   B: all / Not / at / !

   _____

5. **A:** your / profits / comment / on / you / Can / ?

   _____

   B: joking / must / You / be / !

   _____

2 Complete the conversation with the sentences from Exercise 1.

Dana: I'm interviewing Sam Logan. He invented a boat that you pedal and steer like a car. Sam, what was your inspiration for this invention?

Sam: I really like boats and bicycling. So I thought I'd put them together. I was surprised when it worked!

Dana: Sam has produced and sold about 125 of these so far. So, Sam, that seems like a lot to sell.

   1 _____

Sam: Well, Dana. They cost a lot to make, so really, I don't make much on each one. It's just fun for me.

Dana: 2 _____ Is that true?

Sam: 3 _____

   That's funny! I haven't heard from him. But if he does, I will make him a special one!

Dana: It seems like this could be dangerous.

   4 _____

Sam: 5 _____

   That's just a story someone made up! I've never seen any swimming out here. I think the vehicle is kind of large and would scare them.

Dana: Last question, can I take it for a spin?

Sam: 6 _____

   Here, let me show you how to drive it . . .

1 Complete the sentences with the correct phrases.

but I'd also in order to not only so that

1. The thief had to be very quiet _____ not set off the alarms.

2. The thief lied _____ the detective wouldn't think he stole the jewelry.

3. "_____ did I know the thief was lying, _____ guessed where he hid the jewels," said the detective.

2 Complete the text with the phrases from Exercise 1.

MY SECRET

by Harry Sykes

I have a younger brother named Carl. When he was five and I was nine, we used to share the same bedroom. His bedtime was before mine. He would still sleep with his favorite teddy bear in those days. And every night, when I came to bed, I would place his other stuffed animals on his bed. ¹_____ would I put them in there, ²_____ dress them up in his clothing. I had to be very quiet ³_____ not wake him up.

Every morning, he'd wake up to find his stuffed animals wearing his clothing. He thought they got dressed during the night! Then I'd act surprised ⁴_____ he wouldn't suspect I did it. Finally, at breakfast, he'd tell my mother what clothes the toys were wearing. She thought he was making it all up! To this day, I've never admitted what I'd done.

3 Read the text again. Answer the questions.

1. What is the story about?

_____

2. What is the background information?

Who: _____

Where: _____

When: _____

3. What is the order of events?

First: _____

Next: _____

Then: _____

Last: _____

4. How does the story conclude?

_____

1 Cross out the word that doesn't belong in each category.

1. **Preparing for a party:**

   ~~admit something.~~ prepare special food

   dress up put up decorations

2. **Celebrating:**

   write a report have a good time

   hold a contest set off fireworks

3. **Describing a party:**

   crowded lively reply noisy

4. **Describing how people say things:**

   admit claim recommend unsolved

2 Circle the correct words.

1. Juanita **admitted** / **claimed** to telling him about the surprise party.

2. Boris **mentioned** / **insisted** on driving us home after the celebration.

3. Luisa **agreed** / **wrote** to me that the party was a huge success.

4. Amy **agreed** / **told** to help me put up decorations before the party.

5. Ted **recommended** / **replied** to her question by email.

3 Write the quoted speech as reported speech. Use the words in parentheses.

1. Jill: "I told them about the contest." (claim)

   Jill claimed she told them about the contest.

2. Mark: "OK. I'll help you choose some music to play at the party." (agree)

   _____

   _____

3. Brandon: "You're coming to the party!" (insist)

   _____

   _____

4. Olga: "The food at the school festival was pretty good." (say)

   _____

   _____

5. Evan: "I saw them dancing at the party." (mention)

   _____

   _____

4 Complete the text with the correct words.

colorful	messy	~~traditional~~
crowded	noisy	unusual
lively	stunning	

Throw a Great Party!

We asked some teens for ideas on how to make your next party an event to remember. Here's what they said:

- **Alex:** [a]Food is key to having a great event. Serve 1 _traditional_ foods, like sushi, but arrange them in an 2_____ way, for example, to look like a nature scene or a funny face the stranger the better! [b]Remember to have napkins in case things get 3_____!

- **Tracy:** [c]Play 4_____ music to get people dancing! [d]Move the furniture out of the way so the room doesn't feel 5_____. You'll know everyone is having fun when it's so 6_____ you have to talk loudly to be heard over the party!

- **Tom:** [e]Hold a contest! [f]I really enjoy singing contests. Award a prize for the most 7_____ performance. Or make it a costume party. Encourage people to get crazy with their costumes by offering a prize for the brightest and most 8_____ costume.

5 Write the lettered sentences from the text in Activity 4 as reported speech.

a. Alex said _that food is key to having a great event._

b. He also said that _____.

c. Tracy said to _____.

d. She also recommends

_____.

e. Tom suggests _____.

f. He said that _____.

6 Complete the conversations. Use verb + *-ing* form or infinitive.

1. **A:** I don't know what to do for my birthday.
   B: I'd _consider having_ (consider / have) a theme party.

2. **A:** I'm working on the invitation list for my wedding.
   B: Don't _____ (forget / send) them early.

3. **A:** I'm not sure where to have our company party.
   B: If you _____ (decide / have) the party at a restaurant, be sure to call early for a reservation.

4. **A:** I'm planning a karaoke party for my parents!
   B: Not everybody _____ (enjoy / sing) karaoke.

5. **A:** What did you get Jeff for his birthday?
   B: I _____ (try / get) him concert tickets, but they were sold out.

7 Correct the sentences.

1. Before ~~released~~ _releasing_ the official report, the police wanted to make sure it was final.

2. When the detective will have all the facts, she'll reveal who committed the crime.

3. If you look at the map since you go, you won't get lost.

4. After to hide the prize money, the millionaire posted clues on his website so people could try to find it.

5. Jenna always reads the end of the mystery since she finishes the book.

6. Before they made the discovery, they shared their results with other scientists.

8 Complete the conversation.

am so	Not at all!	You must
Great idea!	That's such a	be joking!
~~Is it true that.~~	Yes, absolutely!	

Erin: Hey, Russ. ¹ _Is it true that_ you had a huge party last weekend?

Russ: ² _____
I was studying for my lifeguard test all weekend!

Erin: I was just kidding. But have you heard that I'm planning a big graduation party?

Russ: No way! ³ _____
How do you have time to plan a party with finals coming up?

Erin: I find the time because I want to do it! So get this, our whole class is invited. It'll be a three-day camping trip!

Russ: ⁴ _____
Camping is awesome.

Erin: I know. I
⁵ _____
excited. It's going to be at the lake. Can you be our lifeguard?

Russ: ⁶ _____
I'd be happy to.
⁷ _____
great spot to camp.

Erin: Yeah!

 Weird and Wonderful

VOCABULARY Story elements

1 Find seven more story element words.

O	X	W	G	Z	C	P	M	D	K	S	X	Q	T
B	Z	I	R	A	U	F	M	I	U	R	I	V	E
F	D	D	T	W	W	G	B	J	L	D	R	S	N
M	W	A	V	H	H	Q	V	C	F	S	J	E	D
R	F	O	G	V	L	G	O	F	W	E	I	X	I
M	A	I	N	C	H	A	R	A	C	T	E	R	N
P	Y	C	M	Z	V	Y	U	I	Z	T	T	C	G
E	B	Z	P	A	O	X	A	C	T	I	O	N	F
G	V	I	L	L	A	I	N	R	G	N	G	H	P
D	F	P	L	T	T	G	D	L	C	G	E	W	Q
B	H	G	K	X	Q	S	A	M	H	M	N	L	C
A	N	A	D	W	(P	L	O	T)	Y	B	I	D	K
L	U	O	E	H	E	R	O	M	G	I	Q	Q	R
H	L	W	S	U	S	P	E	N	S	E	K	C	B

2 Replace the underlined phrases with the words and phrases from Exercise 1. Some words will be used more than once.

1. Brenda thinks the *Harry Potter* movies do a good job of keeping the story the same and not changing the ~~things that happened~~. *plot*

2. The book series *Percy Jackson and the Olympians* is named after the <u>important person in the story</u>, Percy Jackson, so we know the books are about him.

3. When they made the movie *Jurassic Park*, they changed the <u>last part of the story</u> from how it was in the book.

4. Tim likes fantasy movies like *The Hobbit* because he likes the <u>place where and when the story happens</u>.

5. Darth Vader, President Coriolanus Snow, and the Joker, are all examples of the <u>bad person in a story</u>.

6. Luke Skywalker, Katniss Everdeen, and Batman are all examples of the <u>good person in a story</u>.

7. Angela wouldn't watch the movie *Jaws* because the <u>feeling of excitement when something is about to happen</u> was too much for her! She said it made her nervous.

8. *Indiana Jones and the Raiders of the Lost Ark* is one of Bill's favorite movies. He loves watching movies with a lot of <u>exciting things happening</u>.

3 Complete the sentences with your own information.

1. My favorite hero in a story is *Spider Man* because *I think it's cool the way he had to learn about power himself.*

   My favorite hero in a story is _____ because _____.

2. My favorite villain in a story is _____ because _____.

3. I don't like it when the main character is _____ because _____ _____.

4. I liked the action in the story _____ because _____ _____.

5. I think the story with the best setting is _____ because _____ _____.

GRAMMAR Third conditional

1 Write third conditional sentences with the information in the chart.

	Imaginary and untrue situation in the past	Impossible consequence
1.	Lesley / not save / the money	she / not buy / a car
2.	You / study	you / do better / on your test than me
3.	Carl / not hear / the noise	he / not lock / the door
4.	Karen and Cindy / not take / photos	no one / believe / their story
5.	Max / go / the beach	he / compete / the swimming contest
6.	I / be nice / to my coach	I / get / more help

1. *If Lesley hadn't saved the money,*

   she wouldn't have bought a car.

2. _____

3. _____

4. _____

5. _____

6. _____

2 Write the questions another way. Then answer the questions with your own information.

1. What would've happened if you had won a million dollars last year?

Q: *If you had won a million dollars last year,*

   what would've happened?

A: *I would have traveled around the world.*

2. What kind of movie would it have been if you had been in a movie?

Q: _____

A: _____

3. If you had helped a friend last year, who would you have helped?

Q: _____

A: _____

4. What celebrity would you have invited if you had had a big birthday party last year?

Q: _____

A: _____

5. If you had known what it would be like, what movie wouldn't you have watched?

Q: _____

A: _____

wish + past perfect

3. Put the words in the correct order to make sentences using *wish* + past perfect.

1. I / I / for / test / wish / studied / the / had / .

   I wish I had studied for the test.

2. gotten / I / sooner / had / wish / I / up / .

   _____

3. run / wishes / had / the / Mike / race / faster / he / in / .

   _____

4. gotten / Kim / had / she / wishes / concert / tickets / .

   _____

5. before / had / we / We / it / rained / left / wish / .

   _____

6. movie / hadn't / wish / heard / how / we / the / ended / We / .

   _____

VOCABULARY Linking phrases

1 Complete the sentences with a word or phrase from each box.

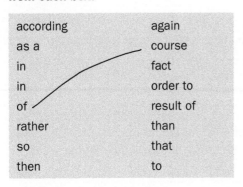

according	again
as a	course
in	fact
in	order to
of	result of
rather	than
so	that
then	to

1. Stephen King was signing books at the bookstore. _____Of course_____, I asked him to sign my copy of his book.

2. Jeanne moved to Hollywood _____ become a movie star.

3. Jonah thought it would be cool to see a ghost, but _____, maybe it wouldn't.

4. Leon could never get to the airport on time, so he bought his own plane _____ miss any more flights.

5. They held the wedding in secret _____ photographers wouldn't spoil their special day.

6. For a long time, Pluto was classified as a planet, when _____, it was really a "dwarf" planet.

7. _____ recent research, the Earth and Moon are 60 million years older than previously thought.

8. She's studied Chinese for years and _____ her studies, she speaks it very well now.

2 Put the words in the correct order to make sentences.

1. visit / most interesting / my friend Juan, / place / Macchu Picchu/ According to / is / the / to / .

   According to my friend Juan, Macchu Picchu
   is the most interesting place to visit.

2. tomato / The / is considered a vegetable, / in / a fruit / fact, / it's / but / .

   _____.

3. formed / result / the hoodoos / of / As a / snow and rain, / were / .

   _____.

4. all / I / marine animals / love / .
   I / swim / with / Of / wouldn't / a shark / want to / course, / !

   _____

   _____

5. movie / video camera / in / to / make / order / John / is / buying / a / a / .

   _____

6. saved / she / money / could / that / Helen / go / college / to / so / .

   _____

7. than / we / a trip / Bryce Canyon, / Rather / took / there / about / just read / .

   _____

GRAMMAR Past modals of speculation

1 Read the sentences. Is the speaker sure or not sure? Check (✓) the correct columns.

	Sure	Not sure
1. Jorge must have been to Mexico City before.	✓	
2. His younger brother couldn't have learned to drive already.		
3. We may have been the first people to see the cave.		
4. Iris might have been at the dance last night.		
5. Henry must not have known that the show was canceled.		
6. They might not have seen this movie before.		

2 **Match the statements with the correct speculations.**

1. Liam wasn't home last night. __*b*__	a. He must have worked hard on it.
2. Tomás didn't go to the free concert last weekend. _____	b. He could have been at his grandmother's.
3. Albert didn't answer his phone. _____	c. He couldn't have completed all of the levels yet.
4. Erik's movie won the school video contest. _____	d. He might have turned it off.
5. Min-Jun got a new car. _____	e. He must not have known about it.
6. Eduard just got that new video game. _____	f. He must be so excited.

3 **Complete the sentences. Use the modals in parentheses and *have* + past participle.**

1. Anna was out in the rain. She *must not have brought* (must not / bring) her umbrella.

2. Paul is tired today. He _____ (might / go) to bed late.

3. Joel didn't ride the roller coaster. He _____ (may / be) too scared.

4. Nicole's car has a flat tire. She _____ (could not / drive) to work today.

5. Alec didn't mention how his band's audition went. It _____ (may not / go) very well.

6. Jin-hee can't find her cat. But it _____ (might not / run) away.

4 **Rewrite the sentences. Use the modals in parentheses and *have* + past participle.**

1. Abby was worried about the test. (could)
   Abby could have been worried about the test.

2. They didn't eat dessert. (must not)
   _____

3. Greg went to the play by himself. (might)
   _____

4. We didn't get good seats in the theater. (could not)
   _____

5. Scientists know why the bees are dying. (must)
   _____

6. I lost my friend's necklace. (may)
   _____

Asking for more information

1. Put the words in the correct order to make sentences and questions.

1. about / Tell / me / it / .

    Tell me about it.

2. happened / What / next / ?

    _____

3. that / Why / was / ?

    _____

4. happened / what / So, / ?

    _____

5. what / next / brilliant / And / then / he / did / was / !

    _____

6. kind / of / what / business / Like / ?

    _____

2 Complete the conversation with the expressions from Exercise 1. More than one answer may be possible.

Jack: I read this really interesting story about Richard Branson last night.

Marnie: Richard Branson, the British businessman? The guy who started Virgin Airlines?
¹ *Tell me about it.*

Jack: Yeah, it's such an amazing story how he started an airline. He was in his late 20s and he had already started one business.

Marnie: ² _____

Jack: It was a business that sold records. He started it in 1972, and it was called Virgin Records. Anyway, one night, he was going to fly to the Virgin Islands in the Caribbean. But his flight was canceled. So he was stuck at the airport.

Marnie: ³ _____

Jack: Because there weren't any more flights that night. But he had to get to the Virgin Islands.

Marnie: ⁴ _____

Jack: He found a private plane that he could "charter," or rent. But he didn't have the money to charter it.

Marnie: ⁵ _____

Jack: He chartered the plane anyway!
⁶ _____

He made a sign that said "Virgin Airlines, $39." And he sold the other seats on the plane to the other passengers who would have been on his canceled flight. After that, he bought the plane!

1 Complete Cesar's story with the adverbs in the box. Sometimes more than one answer is possible.

clearly	Luckily
~~Eventually~~	Obviously
finally	Suddenly
Finally	Unfortunately
fortunately	

The Robot Competition

by Cesar Guerrero

Last weekend, my friend Hiro and I entered a robot in my town's robot competition. We had worked on it for a year. ¹_____*Eventually*_____, it was ready to enter in the contest.

In the competition, each robot got a turn in front of the judges. You had to show what your robot could do. Hiro and I thought our robot was ²_____ the best.

We waited and waited for our turn. The judges ³_____ called our names. Hiro used the remote control to make our robot move. It walked, it spun, it punched. ⁴_____, the robot did everything Hiro commanded it to do. Then I took the controls and made the robot dance. The robot ⁵_____ did everything I wanted it to. ⁶_____, we were very proud of our robot. When our turn was finished, Hiro and I thought we were going to win!

⁷_____, the judges couldn't decide! There was a tie between our robot and another robot. The judges made us perform one more time.

I took the controls and started to make the robot dance. ⁸_____, the robot started to do different things. For several minutes, I tried to make it dance again, but it wouldn't respond to the controls. ⁹_____, it rolled right off the table. Hiro and I lost the competition!

2 Read the story in Exercise 1 again. Look at the adverbs you wrote. Circle the words that show time, underline the words that show opinion, and put a box around the words that state a fact.

3 Read the story in Exercise 1 again. Circle the correct answers.

1. What happens first in the story?
   a. The boys enter their robot in a competition.
   b. The boys become judges.
   c. The boys learn how to make a robot.

2. When did the story happen?
   a. two years ago
   b. last month
   c. last weekend

3. Where did the story happen?
   a. at a robot competition
   b. at a robot club
   c. at a friend's house

4. What happened first?
   a. The robot suddenly stopped working.
   b. Cesar controlled the robot.
   c. The robot performed well.

5. What happened next?
   a. Cesar got mad at Hiro.
   b. Cesar broke the robot.
   c. The robot couldn't be controlled.

6. What happened at the end of the story?
   a. Cesar and Hiro won the competition.
   b. Cesar and Hiro lost the competition.
   c. Cesar and Hiro quit competing.

10 *I Have To!* I Can!

VOCABULARY Training and qualifications

1 Write the collocations. Use a word from each box.

application	course
application	degree
career	exam
college	experience
entrance	fees
training	form
work	path

1. You fill this out to get a job. *application form*

2. This program teaches you the skills you need to do a job. _____

3. You take this test to get into a college or university. _____

4. After you graduate from college, you earn one of these. _____

5. A summer job or internship to gain familiarity with the kind of career you want is this.

   _____

6. When you apply to get into colleges, you often have to pay these. _____

7. This is a series of steps leading to a desired job.

   _____

2 Write the phrases from Exercise 1 in the correct categories. Some may be used more than once.

1. **Things you needed to get into a college or university:**

   _____*application form*_____,

   _____,

   _____

2. **Things you might need to get a job:**

   _____,

   _____

3. **Things that can make up your career path:**

   _____,

   _____

3 Complete the sentences with some of the phrases from Exercise 1.

1. Miranda had to report all her grades and test scores as part of her _____.

2. Dean was surprised that he had to take an _____ for his local college.

3. Nadine knew that gaining _____ in local politics would look good on her résumé.

4. Kim decided not to pursue a _____ and instead started her own company. She wanted to follow a different _____ from her friends.

5. Genevieve was surprised that the _____ _____ required to become a veterinary technician was almost as long as getting a college degree.

6. Joel only applied to his top-three universities because he didn't want to pay any additional

   _____.

4 Answer the questions with your own information.

1. Do you want to get a college degree or go through a training course? Why?

   _____

   _____

2. What kind of work experience do you need for your career path?

   _____

3. What do you think of entrance exams?

   _____

4. Have you ever paid application fees?

   _____

1 **Circle the correct words. Then match the questions with the correct responses.**

1. (Could) / Did he **able to read** / (read) when he was three? _c_

2. **Was / Were** she **able to / managed to** take the entrance exam last weekend? ___

3. How **did / was** he **could / manage** to graduate from high school early? ___

4. What **could / managed** she **do / to do** at 12? ___

5. **Could / Did** he **able to / manage to** get the job? ___

a. He **could / managed to take** extra classes.

b. She **could / able to** speak Russian.

c. Yes, he **able to read / could read** simple books.

d. No, he **didn't / wasn't.** He didn't have enough work experience.

e. Yes, she **was / were.**

2 **Put the words in the correct order to make sentences and questions.**

1. college / you / summer / money / manage / to / / enough / for / save / Did / this / ?

   Did you manage to save enough money for

   college this summer?

2. when / Karen / was / 18, / drive / couldn't / she / .

   _____

3. Cambridge / able / Yuri / to / How / get / accepted / to / was / ?

   _____

4. concert / didn't / manage / win / We / tickets / the / to / to / .

   _____

5. could / she / How / many / play / Nina / was / instruments / five / when / ?

   _____

6. the / they / to / at / able / conference / were / What / learn / ?

   _____

3 **Look at Michael's activities. Complete questions about his past abilities using** *could (not)*, *was/were able to*, **and** *managed to*. **Then answer the questions.**

played music (five instruments)	at age 10
earned money by making digital music and DJing; bought a car	at age 16
played at a famous music festival	one summer while still in school
studied music at a local college; created a music app for smartphones in spare time	after graduating from high school

1. _____Could_____ Michael ___play music___ when he was young?

   _____Yes, he could play five instruments._____

2. How _____ he _____ _____ buy a car at age 16?

   _____

3. What _____ he _____ one summer while he was still in school?

   _____

4. _____ he _____ study music after graduating from high school?

   _____

5. How _____ he _____ _____ create a music app while studying music in college?

   _____

4 **Answer the questions with your own information.**

1. Could you drive when you were 10?

   _____

2. What could you do when you were nine?

   _____

3. Could you speak English very well last year?

   _____

4. What is the most difficult thing you've done? How did you manage to do it?

   _____

VOCABULARY Jobs

1 Look at the pictures and complete the crossword.

across

5.

7.

9.

down

1.

2.

3.

4.

6.

8.

2 Circle the correct answers.

1. Getting a law degree might be good for a career as **an athlete / a chef / a politician.**

2. My cousin is interested in law. He thinks he wants to be a **babysitter / designer / police officer.**

3. Miho loves shopping and clothes. She should just get a job as a **babysitter / politician / salesperson.**

4. Andy has worked at many restaurants over the years. Eventually, he became the head **chef / designer / musician** at a fancy restaurant.

5. When my sister turns 13, she wants to start to work as a **babysitter / police officer / politician.**

6. Arun is creative and has great style. He wants to be **an athlete / a designer / a police officer.**

7. Nancy is great at skiing. She hopes to become a professional **athlete / artist / salesperson.**

8. Graham got a job with the symphony as a **babysitter / musician / politician.** Instead of an entrance exam, he had to perform a solo.

9. My friend is a successful **artist / chef / salesperson.** You can see her work in the museum.

3 Answer the questions with words from Exercise 1 and your own ideas.

1. Which jobs might active people enjoy?

_____

_____

2. Which jobs might creative people enjoy?

_____

3. Which jobs might people who like to work with other people enjoy?

_____

4. Name a famous person for four different jobs:

Job	Name
Athlete	Cristiano Ronaldo

GRAMMAR Modal expressions for past and future

1   Match the questions with the answers.

1. Will you need a degree to be a politician? _e_	a. I'll need to take it by next November.
2. When will you need to take the entrance exam? ____	b. I had to talk to the manager and the owner of the company.
3. How often did you need to practice? ____	c. Yes, I will. But only for the first year.
4. Who did you have to talk to? ____	d. No, I didn't. But there was a fee to take the entrance exam.
5. Will you need to work on weekends? ____	e. No, I won't. But it would help.
6. Did you have to pay an application fee? ____	f. I needed to practice every day.

2   Circle the correct words.

Tara: Hi, Dan. Thanks for answering my questions about medical school. ¹**Did / Had** you ²**have to need / need to take** special classes in college before medical school?

Dan: Yes, I ³**did / had**. Everyone has to take pre-med. It's hard! It's a lot of chemistry, for one thing.

Tara: I've heard that. And what ⁴**did / would** you ⁵**have / have to do** to apply to medical school?

Dan: I ⁶**had to take / would take** the entrance exam. There's a special one for medical school. It's really hard.

Tara: Yeah? And what science classes ⁷**need / will** you ⁸**to take / have to take** when school starts in the fall?

Dan: I ⁹**will have to take / won't have to take** any!

Tara: What? Why?

Dan: Didn't my mom tell you? I got an offer from a soccer league! I can't turn that down! Looks like I ¹⁰**need to be / won't have to be** working on my soccer skills instead!

make and *let*

3   Complete the sentences with the correct form of *make* or *let*.

1. Our English teacher _____made_____ us give speeches so we would be comfortable talking to people.

2. I offered to help, but my parents won't _____ me work at their shop. They want me to spend my time doing homework instead.

3. Sometimes I _____ my friends influence my opinions too much.

4. Tim's school _____ everyone wear uniforms, except on Fridays, when the school _____ students wear what they want.

5. I can't believe Ian _____ you cut his hair! How did you talk him into it?

6. That news program didn't _____ me very happy.

4   Answer the questions with your own information.

1. What is something your teacher makes you do?

   My teacher makes me rewrite every paper.

2. What is something parents usually make their young children do?

   _____

3. What is something you have to make yourself do?

   _____

4. What do your friend's parents let him or her do?

   _____

5. What is something your parents will let you do when you're older?

   _____

6. What do you wish your school would let you do?

   _____

1 Match the phrases to make sentences.

1. How about _c_

2. Why ____

3. I've made up ____

4. That depends on ____

5. Ben might change his mind ____

6. Although, on second thought, ____

a. maybe we should make them see each other.

b. about coming on the hike.

c. going on a hike with him?

d. my mind.

e. the weather.

f. not?

2 Complete the conversation with the sentences from Exercise 1.

Doris: What should we do this weekend?

Frank: Ben is around this weekend. [1] _How about going on a hike with him?_

Doris: [2] _____
I heard it might rain. Also, I'm not sure about letting Ben coming with us.

Frank: [3] _____

Doris: Well, I told Sophia she could do something with us this weekend.

Frank: Oh, right. If Sophia's coming, [4] _____.

Doris: Yeah, he might. [5] _____ Then they'd have to get along.

Frank: I'm not sure that's a good idea.

Doris: You know what? [6] _____ I think we should have a big party. Then everyone will *have* to get along.

Frank: That might work.

Doris: Yeah, and if it doesn't, it might be interesting anyways!

1 Complete the sentences with *either . . . or* or *neither . . . nor.*

1. Jenny doesn't like peanut butter. And she doesn't like jelly.

   Jenny likes _____ peanut butter _____ jelly.

2. Misha wants to learn to play the violin. But if he can't play that, he'd be happy with piano.

   Misha wants to play _____ the violin _____ the piano.

2 Read the text. Then rewrite the underlined sentences using *either . . . or* or *neither . . . nor.*

Do you know Ella Marija Lani Yelich-O'Connor? Here's a hint: ¹She is not an actor. She is not a fashion designer. She's a singer. ²She is not from Australia. And she is not from the U.K. She's from New Zealand. She's under 25. Her stage name is one word. Guessed it yet?

If you guessed the pop singer Lorde, you're correct!

Lorde was interested in performing as a young girl. She was in drama school at the age of five. Her mother let her read all kinds of books as a child. When she was 13, her band won the school's talent show. When she was 15, she took singing lessons twice a week and also began writing songs. Eventually, she released a record, and the single "Royals" became a number-one hit in the United States in 2012, making Lorde the youngest singer to do that since 1988. Her debut album from 2013 was nominated for a Grammy Award. "Tennis Court" and "Glory and Gore" were hit songs from that album. She has also written songs for the *Hunger Games* movies soundtrack.

How does she sound? She doesn't play any instruments, so she uses her voice to carry the story of her songs. ³ So you could call her voice intriguing. Some says it's mysterious. What type of music is it? ⁴ I'd say her music is pop. Or it's electro. In 2013, *Time* magazine named her one of the most influential teenagers in the world. We can't wait to hear more from her!

1. _____
2. _____
3. _____
4. _____

3 Read the text again. Answer the questions.

1. What is Lorde's real name?

   _____

2. Where is she from?

   _____

3. What type of music does she play?

   _____

4. When and how did she start?

   _____

5. What are some of her hit songs?

   _____

6. What are some interesting facts about her?

   _____

1 Look at the pictures and complete the puzzle. Then use the words in grey to solve the riddle.

(crossword grid with numbered entries 1a, 1b, 2, 3, 4, 5, 6, 7, 8 and letter N)

I am not an athlete, but I have to "run" for office. What job do I have?

1a. and 1b. (two words).

2. 3. 4. 5. 6. 7. 8.

2 Put the words in the correct order to make sentences.

1. have / Soren / to / entrance / take / Did / an / exam / ?

_____

2. work / get / did / need / you / experience / to / What / ?

_____

3. will / take / Jun Hee / When / training / to / have / the / course / ?

_____

4. application / Kelly / had / forms / to / fill / seven / out / .

_____

5. degree / have / college / to / Will / earn / a / Josh / ?

_____

6. didn't / I / to / path / on / need / a / career / decide / .

_____

3 Complete the sentences with the correct forms of *let* or *make*.

1. Our boss doesn't _____ us fill out time sheets.

2. That training course we took last month _____ us see police officers in a new way.

3. My parents won't _____ me drive until I'm 18!

4. My parents _____ me play computer games as often as I like, as long as my grades are good.

4 Complete the article with the correct words.

According to	In fact
~~as a result of.~~	Rather than
in order to	so that

Hope LeVin

Who is Hope LeVin? She's a professional athlete. She grew up in the Turks and Caicos Islands in the Caribbean. She used to watch kiteboarders on the beach when she was growing up.

When she was 11, someone asked her if she'd like to learn how. She said yes, and [1] *as a result* of that decision, she grew up to become a professional kiteboarder! [2] _____ being an overnight success, Hope had to work hard for many years. She kited every day, but for the first couple of months, she could only ride in one direction. She kept practicing [3] _____, eventually, she could ride in both directions. [4] _____ Hope, you have to be really patient [5] _____ learn kiteboarding.

In 2013, she entered a kiteboarding competition in the Dominican Republic. She didn't expect to do well, but [6] _____, she managed to win second place! That was when she decided to turn pro.

When Hope isn't kiting, competing, or spreading the word of kiteboarding, she's studying for a long-distance degree in economics. That's Hope LeVin, flying high!

5 Circle the correct words.

Lois: Hi Emi! Did you hear what happened to Carl?

Emi: No, ¹(tell me about it) / like what?

Lois: He went to the city and tried out for that reality show for musicians.

Emi: That's great! ²**So, what happened? / In fact?**

Lois: Well, he wasn't going to audition at all. But his friend Dylan, who's in his band, got him to ³**on second thought / change his mind**. So he went along with Dylan to the audition. He was thinking, ⁴**"Why was that / Why not** give it a try?" But then he said he almost didn't go through with it.

Emi: ⁵**On second thought. / Why was that?**

Lois: He said when they got there, there was only one spot left to audition. Dylan wanted it. And so did a bunch of other kids. They were all standing in line waiting to be chosen. So Carl ⁶**made up his mind / that depends on** that he'd let Dylan have the spot. And he went off to the side and just started listening to his headphones and dancing and singing to himself.

Emi: ⁷**And then what happened? / Like what?**

Lois: Well, one of the show's producers saw him dancing and singing to himself and she came over to him. She said, "⁸**How about / That depends on** if you take the last spot to audition?"

Emi: Oh my gosh! What did he do?

Lois: He said he looked over at Dylan and Dylan encouraged him, so he said yes! He's going to be on the show!

6 Read the conversation in Exercise 5 again. Imagine that Carl's audition was really a short story that Lois wrote. Answer the questions.

1. Who is the main character of the story?

   _____

2. What is the setting of the story?

   _____

3. In the story, was Dylan a hero, a villain, or neither? Why?

   _____

4. What was the plot of the story?

   _____

   _____

5. What happened at the end of the story?

   _____

   _____

7 Complete the sentences about Exercise 5. Use the words in parentheses to make the third conditional or past modals of speculation.

1. If Dylan hadn't invited him, Carl *wouldn't have gone to the audition* . (go /audition)

2. If Carl had stayed in line, _____. (might not / choose)

3. If Carl hadn't been singing and dancing on the side, the producer _____. (may not / notice)

4. But if Carl had stayed in line, he _____. (could not / be seen)

5. I bet Dylan _____ he _____ in line. (wish / had not / stay)

6. I wonder if Dylan _____ he _____ Carl to come to the audition! (wish / had not / ask)

Real or FAKE?

BEFORE YOU WATCH

1 Answer these questions about how you use the Internet.

1. What websites do you use to get information? Name two. _____

2. Can you tell if a digital photo has been edited? How? _____

WHILE YOU WATCH

2 Watch the video. Are the sentences true (*T*) or false (*F*)? Correct the false sentences.

1. Until recently, people got most of their information from books. _____

2. In the past, it was easy to share visual information with a lot of people. _____

3. Today, anyone can claim to be an expert. _____

4. It's very easy now to manipulate visual information. _____

5. Only experts can decide if something is real or fake. _____

3 Watch the video again. Complete the sentences with the words you hear.

1. It used to take a lot of time and _____ to share information with a lot of people.

2. Books were usually _____ by _____.

3. But can you believe everything you _____ or _____?

4. They are controlling the _____ so you will _____ their product.

5. You just have to _____ attention and not _____ everything you see or read.

AFTER YOU WATCH

4 Work with a partner. Think about where you get your information. Do you trust what you read? Why or why not?

> I go on Wikipedia sometimes to research historical events. But I know that anyone can post on Wikipedia, so I always check another source.

Milan's FASHION WEEK

BEFORE YOU WATCH

1 Look at the pictures and the sentences from the video. Complete the sentences with the correct words, then match the sentences to the pictures.

a.

b.

c.

> make-up   patterns   photographers

1. Lots of _____ come to Milan for Fashion Week.   _____

2. The designer Missoni is famous for his bold _____.   _____

3. It takes hours to do each model's hair and _____!   _____

WHILE YOU WATCH

2 Watch the video. Are the sentences true (*T*) or false (*F*)? Correct the false sentences.

1. The blogger got a chance to go to Milan recently. _____

2. Missoni often uses bright colors in his designs. _____

3. The blogger thinks it would be cool to be a model. _____

4. A lot of the models had long hair. _____

5. There was a big dinner after the show. _____

3 Watch the video again. Answer the questions.

1. What does the blogger call Milan? _____

2. Who is one of the blogger's favorite designers? _____

3. Why is there a lot of waiting around before the show? _____

4. What does the blogger not have patience for? _____

5. What do the models do at the end of the show? _____

AFTER YOU WATCH

4 Work in small groups. Discuss how fashions have changed in the past five years. What were styles you used to think were cool, but now you'd never wear?

> A few years ago, I used to wear really baggy jeans and big hats. I thought hoodies in really bright colors were cool – but not anymore!

Born to DIVE

BEFORE YOU WATCH

1 Look at these pictures from the video of a free diver. Do you think the statements are true (*T*) or false (*F*)?

1. Free divers dive underwater on one breath of air. _____

2. Some professional free divers use equipment to help them breathe underwater. _____

3. Some free divers can stay underwater for three minutes or longer. _____

WHILE YOU WATCH

2 Watch the video. Circle the correct answers.

1. Which adjective best describes Michele?

   a. shy   b. determined   c. impatient

2. To become a professional diver, Michele must dive to a depth of more than _____ meters.

   a. 45   b. 50   c. 55

3. Michele's parents are _____ him.

   a. worried about   b. angry with   c. afraid of

4. Michele says his mother _____ what he does.

   a. is happy about   b. doesn't understand   c. doesn't like

5. Michele reaches _____ meters in the competition.

   a. 57   b. 67   c. 47

3 Watch the video again. Check (✓) the sentences you hear.

1. ❑   Fear is something you don't need.

2. ❑   I'm not scared because I know my limits.

3. ❑   On the day of the championship, there are big crowds.

4. ❑   He dives deep very fast.

5. ❑   His dream has finally come true!

AFTER YOU WATCH

4 Work with a partner. Discuss: Do you know anyone who has hurt themselves doing a sport? What happened?

> Well, my brother broke his leg skiing a few years ago. He was going down a hill, and he hit a tree.

Shanghai HEIGHTS

BEFORE YOU WATCH

1 Look at this picture from the video. Answer the questions.

1. Where is this man and what is he doing? _____

2. Would you like to have his job? Why or why not? _____

WHILE YOU WATCH

2 Watch the video. Match the phrases to make true sentences.

1. Many people come to Shanghai _____   a. for months.

2. Sun Feng cleans the windows _____   b. to hold his daughter.

3. He has not seen his family   _____   c. by train.

4. He travels to his village   _____   d. to find jobs.

5. He is very happy   _____   e. of tall buildings.

3 Watch the video again. Answer the questions.

1. Why did Sun Feng move to Shanghai? _____

2. What does he say is the worst thing about the job? _____

3. How did he feel the first time he did the job? _____

4. What does he bring home for everyone? _____

5. What does he give his father at dinner? _____

AFTER YOU WATCH

4 Work in small groups. Discuss: Would you ever take a job far from home? What kind of job would that be?

> Yes, I would. I would take a job that was really interesting and paid a lot of money. I'd also like to live in another country.

What A WASTE!

BEFORE YOU WATCH

1 Look at these pictures from the video. Answer the questions.

1. What do you think is going to happen to these old computers? _____

2. The picture on the right is of a *landfill* – a large trash site. What do you think the people are doing there? _____

WHILE YOU WATCH

2 Watch the video. Answer the questions.

1. What is the first example of things we throw away each year? _____

2. How many cell phones do Americans throw away each day? _____

3. How many kilos of oil does it take to make one computer screen? _____

4. What could we do with our old computers? _____

5. What kind of phone is much cheaper than a new one? _____

3 Watch the video again. Circle the words you hear.

BILL NYE: What is e-waste?

MAN 1:   Um, waste . . . **electricity / electric** that's wasted?

WOMAN 1: E-waste? **Ecology / Ecological** waste or something?

BILL NYE: Do you know what e-waste is?

WOMAN 2: Oh, maybe it's the **economic / economical** waste. Maybe like from the economy?

MAN 2:   **Environment / Environmental** waste?

AFTER YOU WATCH

4 Work with a partner. Make a list of all your electronic devices. What will you do with them when they get old? Think of ways you could reduce your personal e-waste.

Device	To do
cell phone	*donate to a charity*
printer	*return to manufacturer to recycle*

Mission: POSSIBLE?

BEFORE YOU WATCH

1 Read the sentences. Write the letter of the correct definition of the underlined words.

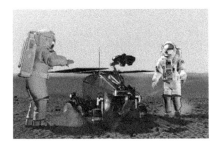

1. Will <u>astronauts</u> ever travel to Mars? _____

2. Some people feel <u>motion sickness</u> when they try to read in a car. _____

3. Many emergency vehicles have <u>flashing</u> lights to warn people of danger. _____

a. something that appears quickly or suddenly

b. a person who travels in a spacecraft to outer space

c. a type of nausea

WHILE YOU WATCH

2 Watch the video. Are the sentences true (*T*) or false (*F*)? Correct the false sentences.

1. Scientists have mastered time travel. _____

2. Traveling in space makes some astronauts sick. _____

3. The professor invented special books for astronauts to read. _____

4. One woman wore normal, clear glasses. _____

5. The woman with the flashing glasses felt good. _____

3 Watch the video again. Answer the questions.

1. What do many astronauts suffer from? _____

2. What was unusual about the eyes of the one astronaut? _____

3. What was the difference between the glasses the two women wore?

   _____

4. What were the women doing in the car? _____

5. Which woman became sick? _____

AFTER YOU WATCH

4 Work in small groups. Discuss: Do you think humans will travel to other planets in your lifetime? Where will they go first? Would you want to travel in space?

> I think humans will go to Mars in my lifetime. Yes, I would want to travel in space, but it could be scary.

The ORIGIN OF ARGAN OIL

BEFORE YOU WATCH

1 Look at the picture from the video. Answer the questions.

1. Where are these goats and what are they doing? _____

2. What are some foods we get from goats? _____

WHILE YOU WATCH

2 Watch the video. Answer the questions.

1. What is strange about the argan trees? _____

2. What are the goats doing? _____

3. What colors are the goats? _____

4. What do people make argan oil from? _____

5. What do people use argan oil for? _____

3 Watch the video again. Put the steps of making argan oil in order.

1. First, _____   a. women roast the argan seeds over a fire.

2. Then, _____   b. they make a paste from the seeds.

3. Then, _____   c. goats eat argan fruit from a tree.

4. Next, _____   d. the women make a delicate oil.

5. Finally, _____   e. the argan fruit passes through the goats' bodies.

AFTER YOU WATCH

4 Work with a partner. Make a list of at least three animals and what humans get from them.

Animal	Product
goat	milk
	cheese
	meat
	leather

Fruits of the SEA

BEFORE YOU WATCH

1 Look at these pictures from the video. Complete the sentences with the correct words.

good	islands	protein	seafood

Japan is a group of ¹_____ surrounded by the sea. People here eat a lot of ²_____.
Fish is very ³_____ for you. It's full of ⁴_____ and vitamins. Fishing is essential to life in
these islands.

WHILE YOU WATCH

2 Watch the video. Circle the correct words.

1. In the first half of the video, most of the people are **young / old**.

2. Japanese people eat **10 percent / 10 tons** of all the fish caught in the world.

3. Fishermen catch squid **at night / in the morning**.

4. One of the most popular fish in Japan is the **abalone / bluefin tuna**.

5. Every day, over **40,000 / 400,000** buyers come to the Tokyo fish market.

3 Watch the video again. Check (✔) the sentences you hear.

1. ❑ Rich water. Water that is full of fish.

2. ❑ Life expectancy here is over 80 years old.

3. ❑ Further in, you can find squid.

4. ❑ Bluefin tuna swim in the deep waters of northern Japan.

5. ❑ There's no question of Japan's love for the sea.

AFTER YOU WATCH

4 Work in small groups. Discuss: Do you eat a lot of seafood? What are your favorite types? If you don't eat
seafood, what are other sources of protein in your diet?

> I eat seafood about once a week. My favorite is
> shrimp. I also like fried fish.

A COOL EXPERIMENT

BEFORE YOU WATCH

1 Look at this graphic of global warming from the video. Do you think the sentences are true (*T*) or false (*F*)?

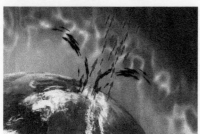

1. Many scientists say temperatures around the world are rising. _____

2. Greenhouse gases such as CO_2 and methane cool the Earth's environment. _____

3. Humans produce greenhouse gases. _____

WHILE YOU WATCH

2 **Watch the video. Complete the sentences.**

1. Eric is going to build _____ greenhouses, each with an _____ statue.

2. He's going to fill _____ of the greenhouses with _____ air.

3. Each box will receive the same _____ of _____.

4. Computers will monitor the amount of _____ in the _____.

5. Eric _____ to be part of the _____.

3 **Watch the video again. Circle any wrong words. Write the correct words on the lines.**

Ex.: First, he looked at the ⟨scientist⟩ behind it. _____*science*_____

1. Each box must be the same. _____

2. He'll fill one box with CO_2, two with methane, and one with normal air. _____

3. They'll need special machines to make the ice boxes. _____

4. After four-and-a-half hours, the ice statues start to melt! _____

5. Methane and CO_2 are major culprits for global warming. _____

AFTER YOU WATCH

4 **Work in small groups. Discuss: Do temperatures seem to be rising where you live? Are there more storms and floods where you live than there were several years ago?**

> I'm not sure. I think temperatures are a little warmer. We did have two big storms last year. My aunt's house was flooded.

Trendsetters

BEFORE YOU WATCH

1 Look at these pictures from the video and read the definition. Then answer the question.

Trendsetter /'trend' setər/ (noun)
a person, organization, etc., that starts to do something that others then copy

These girls are *trendsetters* in Japan. Think of a recent trend in your school. How and where did it start?

_____

WHILE YOU WATCH

2 Watch the video. Circle the correct adverbs.

1. In Japan, trends are **nearly / really** vital.

2. The opinions of trendsetters are **slightly / extremely** important to companies.

3. The girls are **absolutely / somewhat** impressed by the video booth.

4. They think that the photo booth is **pretty / slightly** easier to use.

5. The girls are **very / hardly** excited to meet their friends.

3 Watch the video again. Answer the questions.

1. Where do the two girls live? _____

2. What do companies in Japan want to know? _____

3. What are the girls testing today? _____

4. Which booth do the girls prefer? _____

5. Why do companies care what Saeko and Yuko think about new products?

_____

AFTER YOU WATCH

4 Work with a partner. Make an advertisement for a new trend, such as a new style of shoes or a new smart device. Include graphics and text. Share your advertisement with the class.

Survival OBJECTS

BEFORE YOU WATCH

1 Look at the pictures from the video and read the sentences. Write the letter of the correct definition of each underlined word.

1. The man fills his <u>parachute</u> with snow so he doesn't fall down the mountains. _____

2. He sleeps in a <u>cave</u> in the snow. _____

3. There can be <u>cracks</u> in the ice beneath the deep snow that are very dangerous. _____

a. a piece of equipment that allows a person to fall slowly through the air when dropped from an aircraft

b. a very narrow break or opening in something

c. a large hole in the ground or in a hill

WHILE YOU WATCH

2 Watch the video. Answer the questions.

1. Why does Bear have to be careful in the beginning of the video? _____

2. How does he make his snow cave? _____

3. How does he get water to drink? _____

4. How does he stay warm at night? _____

5. What does he have to do in the morning to find food and keep warm?

_____

3 Watch the video again. Are the sentences true (*T*) or false (*F*)? Correct the false sentences.

1. Bear uses his backpack to dig in the snow. _____

2. During the night, Bear gets covered with water. _____

3. In the morning, there's nothing to eat. _____

4. In the trees, he finds fruit to eat. _____

5. The tea he makes has a lot of orange juice. _____

AFTER YOU WATCH

4 Work with a partner. Imagine that there is a fire in your home. You must leave in five minutes. What three things would you take with you?

I'd definitely take my cat. And my phone . . . and my iPad!

The START OF THE WEB

BEFORE YOU WATCH

1 Write sentences using at least three of the words below.

| cell phone | message | network | text | web | wireless |

1. _____

2. _____

3. _____

WHILE YOU WATCH

2 Watch the video. Answer the questions.

1. In the early days, where did most people use the Internet? _____

2. What did computers look like in the 1960s? _____

3. Who used computers in the 1960s? _____

4. When was the first email sent? _____

5. How did computers change in the 1980s and 1990s? _____

3 Watch the video again. Are the sentences true (T) or false (F)? Correct the false sentences.

1. Computers have always communicated with each other._____

2. ARPANET was one of the first computer networks. _____

3. Computer networks have become smaller and cheaper. _____

4. Web pages and chat rooms became popular in the 1960s. _____

5. We can expect the Internet to continue growing. _____

AFTER YOU WATCH

4 Work in small groups. Complete the chart. Discuss: What websites did you like two years ago? What websites do you like now?

Websites I liked two years ago	Websites I like now
Facebook	Tumblr

Let's CELEBRATE

BEFORE YOU WATCH

1 Look at the picture from the video. Answer the question.

This is a celebration in China. What festivals or holidays do people celebrate with fireworks in your country?

_____

WHILE YOU WATCH

2 Watch the video. Complete the phrases with the name of the correct country, then match them with phrases a–d to make true sentences.

1. People in _____China_____ celebrate New Year's by _____

2. In winter, many people in _____ like to _____

3. In _____, spring is a time for _____

4. Autumn in _____ is when people celebrate _____

a. swim in outdoor pools.

b. Diwali.

c. watching cherry blossoms and picnicking.

d. lighting fireworks.

3 Watch the video again. Complete the sentences with the words you hear.

1. People all over the world enjoy celebrating the changing _____.

2. In China, _____ marks the beginning of a _____.

3. It's a time for visiting _____ and _____.

4. In Japan, _____ is the time of renewal.

5. In India, it's Diwali – the festival of _____ and the beginning of a _____ year.

AFTER YOU WATCH

4 Work in small groups. Discuss: How do you mark the changing of seasons? Do you wear different clothes, eat different foods, or do different things in each season?

> In the summer, I wear shorts and T-shirts and I go swimming almost every day. In the winter, I stay inside!

Like FATHER, LIKE DAUGHTER

BEFORE YOU WATCH

1 Look at the picture from the video. Answer the questions.

What is this person doing? Where do you think he is? _____

WHILE YOU WATCH

2 Watch the video. Circle the correct words to complete the sentences.

1. The first cliff divers were **fishermen / boaters**.

2. For nearly **88 / 80** years, only men were cliff divers.

3. José Luis is called "The Knife" because his dives are so **strong / precise**.

4. Iris's mother says that **diving / school** is first.

5. Before she dives, Iris feels **nervous / peaceful**.

3 Watch the video again. Answer the questions.

1. What is Acapulco famous for? _____

2. What did the fishermen challenge each other to do? _____

3. What tradition is Iris ready to change? _____

4. When does Iris practice diving? _____

5. How high is Iris's dive today? _____

AFTER YOU WATCH

4 Work with a partner. Discuss: What sports used to be only for men, but now are for women, too? What sports still do not include women?

> Soccer and basketball used to be only for men. I don't think there are any women playing football …

A LOST CIVILIZATION

BEFORE YOU WATCH

1 Look at the pictures from the video and read the definitions. Complete the sentences with the correct words.

1. A worker removes a body from a _____ in the desert.

2. This _____ had been _____ for more than 700 years.

3. They found _____ such as this gold pitcher in the graves.

4. Some of the hats they found had the feathers of _____ birds.

artifacts: objects that were made by people long ago

grave: a place where a dead person is buried

mummy: a dead body that has been preserved

preserved: kept from decay; kept in its original condition

tropical: from the tropics (the hottest area on Earth)

WHILE YOU WATCH

2 Watch the video. Circle the correct words.

1. The Atacama Desert is next to the **Atlantic / Pacific** Ocean.
2. The bodies were preserved by the dry, **salty / heavy** sand.
3. Today there are **a few / no** buildings in the area.
4. Many graves had one or two **human / animal** heads.
5. The Amazon Forest is **near / far from** the Atacama Desert.

3 Watch the video again. Answer the questions.

1. What did workers discover in Peru about 15 years ago? _____
2. When did the Chiribaya live in the Ilo Valley? _____
3. How many people probably lived there? _____
4. Where did they get wool for their clothes? _____
5. Where might the tropical feathers have come from? _____

AFTER YOU WATCH

4 What do you think life was like where you live 2,000 years ago? How many people lived there? What animals and plants lived there? Draw a picture, and then describe it to a partner.

> So, 2,000 ago, about 1,000 people lived here. There were rabbits and bears and chickens. There were more trees and plants.

Mysteries OF THE BRAIN

BEFORE YOU WATCH

1 **Look at this picture from the video. Do you think the statements are true (*T*) or false (*F*)?**

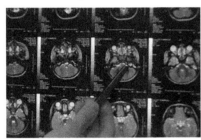

1. Scientists now understand how the brain works. _____

2. When something goes wrong with the brain, scientists can predict what will happen. _____

3. Each part of your brain has a different job. _____

WHILE YOU WATCH

2 **Watch the video. Match the phrases to make true sentences.**

1. When Michael was 10, he _____   a. was damaged.

2. A few years later, scientists _____   b. became interested in art.

3. They found that not all parts of his brain _____   c. were advanced.

4. Dr. Jill Taylor's brain _____   d. graduated from college.

5. After she was in the hospital, Jill _____   e. studied his brain.

3 **Watch the video again. Correct the mistake in the sentences.**

                                body

1. We can do amazing things when our mind and ~~hands~~ work together. _____

2. Michael does very well answering the doctors' questions about words and faces. _____

3. We know that the same parts of the brain control how we think and feel. _____

4. Dr. Jill Bolte Taylor was doing research on the human body. _____

5. We don't have many unanswered questions about the brain. _____

AFTER YOU WATCH

4 **Work with a small group. Think about the different ways of learning. How do you prefer to learn something – by seeing, hearing, or doing?**

> I like learning by seeing. I can remember things better if I can visualize the image in a book or the word on a page.

On THE RUN

Unit 9 Video 9.1

BEFORE YOU WATCH

1 Look at these pictures from the video. Circle the correct answers.

1. This man probably lives _____.

   a. with his family   b. by himself   c. with his friends

2. He probably _____.

   a. works in an office   b. goes to school   c. neither a. or b.

3. He probably has _____.

   a. cheated on a test   b. done something illegal   c. lied to his friend

WHILE YOU WATCH

2 Watch the video. Match the phrases to make true sentences.

1. First, Jamey stole   _____   a. cars.

2. Then, he stole   _____   b. police.

3. When he was 18, he began stealing _____   c. chickens.

4. Then, he hid from the   _____   d. a horse.

3 Watch the video again. Answer the questions.

1. When did Jamey's crimes begin? _____

2. What did his best friend say about Jamey's actions? _____

3. Where did Jamey hide after he stole a car? _____

4. What did his mother tell him to do? _____

5. Where did the police find Jamey? _____

6. Where is Jamey now? _____

AFTER YOU WATCH

4 Complete this chart about Jamey. Then work with a partner. Compare what you wrote. Did you see and hear the same things?

Physical description	
What he thinks / says	
What he does	
What other people say about him	

Insectmobile

BEFORE YOU WATCH

1 Look at the picture from the video. Answer the questions.

What do you think this object is? What is its function? _____

_____

WHILE YOU WATCH

2 Watch the video. Match the phrases to make true sentences.

1. The scientists get a flat tire and they _____   a. are really stable.

2. To learn more about insects, they _____   b. build a prototype.

3. They learn that insects with six legs _____   c. test the real vehicle.

4. Then, they _____   d. decide that legs may be better than wheels.

5. Finally, they _____   e. go to a university to talk to an expert.

3 Watch the video again. Circle the correct adverbs.

1. The scientists are driving when **finally / suddenly** they get a flat tire.

2. The broken wheel **actually / really** gives them some new ideas.

3. They decide that **clearly / slightly** there's a reason creatures have legs instead of wheels.

4. **Fortunately / Unfortunately**, they find an expert on insects at the university.

5. **Finally / Suddenly**, they build a vehicle and test it.

AFTER YOU WATCH

4 Work with a small group. Discuss: How would you improve an object you use every day, such as your phone or your car?

> Well, I'd make my phone do everything my computer can do. I'd make my car respond to voice commands. I'd also make the seats more comfortable.

Future DIRECTIONS

BEFORE YOU WATCH

1 Look at these pictures from the video. Answer the questions.

1. What do you think this woman's job might be? _____

2. Like most people in China, she is an only child. How do you think being an only child affects her relationship with her parents? _____

WHILE YOU WATCH

2 Watch the video. Answer the questions.

1. How does Jolene start each day? _____

2. What does Jolene say about herself? _____

3. What are her two jobs? _____

4. What do her parents think of her career? _____

5. What does she sometimes worry about? _____

3 Watch the video again. Match the columns to make phrases from the video.

1. feel _____   a. as an equal

2. have _____   b. a different path in life

3. make _____   c. positive about

4. take _____   d. the guts to

5. treat _____   e. a contribution to

AFTER YOU WATCH

4 Work in a small group. Make a list of at least three jobs that used to be done only by men or only by women, but are now done by both sexes. Why were these jobs done only by men or by women? Discuss your lists.

> Well, soldiers used to be only men because it was a dangerous job. The leaders of many countries have usually been men, but today, it is more common for women to be in positions of power, too.

The Young *and the* BRAVE

BEFORE YOU WATCH

1 Look at the pictures from the video. Answer the questions.

1. What do you think these children are doing and why? _____

2. What reward might they get for doing this? _____

WHILE YOU WATCH

2 Watch the video. Complete the sentences.

1. Inner Mongolia has thousands of kilometers of grasslands and _____.

2. They play the same games today that they played _____ ago.

3. The children had to train for the race for _____.

4. They ride their horses without _____.

5. When their horses get tired, the children _____ to them.

3 Watch the video again. Answer the questions.

1. What abilities are Mongols famous for? _____

2. When do many Mongol children learn how to ride horses? _____

3. How old are the children in the horse race? _____

4. How long is the race? _____

5. Who wins the race? _____

AFTER YOU WATCH

4 Work with a partner. Discuss: Are there certain things that children do better than adults? Why?

> Children are usually better with technology than adults are. I think children can learn things on a computer faster than adults because they're not afraid of technology.

Notes

Notes

Credits

The authors and publishers acknowledge the following sources of copyright material and are grateful for the permissions granted. While every effort has been made, it has not always been possible to identify the sources of all the material used, or to trace all copyright holders. If any omissions are brought to our notice, we will be happy to include the appropriate acknowledgements on reprinting.

p. 5 (BL): Alamy/©Jan Wlodarczyk; p. 7 (CL): Getty Images/Henrik Sorensen; p. 9 (BL): Getty Images/Zoranm; p. 15 (TL): Shutterstock/Testing; p. 16 (TL): Shutterstock/CandyBox Images; p. 17 (CL): Getty Images/M-imagephotography/iStockphoto; p. 18 (A): Getty Images/Hero Images; p. 18 (B): Shuttertstock/Jianghaistudio; p. 18 (C): Shutterstock/Halfpoint; p. 18 (D): Getty Images/Joel Eichler; p. 18 (E): Getty Images/Mark Bowden; p. 18 (F): Alamy/©Hero Images Inc.; p. 18 (G): Shutterstock/William Perugini; p. 18 (H): Shutterstock/Bikeriderlondon; p. 21 (CR): Shutterstock/Sean Locke Photography; p. 22 (1): Shutterstock/Yuriy Rudyy; p. 22 (2): Shutterstock/Photographee.eu; p. 22 (3): Shutterstock/Sergey Ryzhov; p. 22 (4): Shutterstock/Iakov Filimonov; p. 22 (5): Shutterstock/Photographee.eu; p. 22 (6): Shutterstock/ffolas; p. 22 (7): Shutterstock/Africa Studio; p. 22 (8): Getty Images/Ryerson Clark; p. 22 (9): Getty Images/Dennis Hoyne; p. 23 (TR): Shutterstock/Jacek Chabraszewski; p. 27 (CR): Shutterstock/Ulga; p. 30 (CL): Getty Images/PhotoAlto/Frederic Cirou; p. 31 (CL): Shutterstock/Konrad Mostert; p. 35 (C): Getty Images/DreamPictures; p. 36 (1): Shutterstock/Nickolay Khoroshkov; p. 36 (2): Shutterstock/R. MACKAY PHOTOGRAPHY, LLC; p. 36 (3): Shutterstock/Nikita Rogul; p. 36 (4): Getty Images/phanlop888/iStockphoto; p. 36 (5): Shutterstock/Maggee; p. 36 (6): Shutterstock/Africa Studio; p. 36 (7): Shutterstock/Mdblk1984; p. 36 (8): Shutterstock/Olga Kovalenko; p. 36 (9): Shutterstock/Olga Popova; p. 36 (10): Alamy/©Corbis Super; p. 41 (TR): Shutterstock/Igor Lateci; Shutterstock/sunlight77; p. 46 (CL): Shutterstock/PAUL ATKINSON; p. 47 (CR): Alamy/©Renato Granieri; p. 50 (TR): Alamy/©David Parker; p. 62 (CT): Getty Images/Andy Shaw/Bloomberg; p. 63 (CL): Alamy/©Paolo Patrizi; p. 69 (CR): Alamy/©ZUMA Press, Inc.; p. 70 (1): Alamy/©Gabe Palmer; p. 70 (2): Shutterstock/Valeriy Velikov; p. 70 (3): Getty Images/Steve Debenport; p. 70 (4): Shutterstock/Stasique; p. 70 (5): Alamy/©fStop Images GmbH; p. 70 (6): Shutterstock/Rido; p. 70 (7): Shutterstock/scyther5; p. 70 (8): Shutterstock/Andrey_Popov.

Front cover photography by Alamy/©Image Source Plus.

The publishers are grateful to the following illustrators:
Q2A Media Services, Inc.

All video stills by kind permission of Discovery Communications, LLC 2015.